T0324278

As If

As If

Idealization and Ideals

Kwame Anthony Appiah

Harvard University Press

Cambridge, Massachusetts
London, England

2017

Library of Congress Cataloging-in-Publication Data

Names: Appiah, Anthony, author.
Title: As if : idealization and ideals / Kwame Anthony Appiah.
Description: Cambridge, Massachusetts : Harvard University
    Press, 2017. | Includes bibliographical references and index.
Identifiers: LCCN 2017006995 | ISBN 9780674975002 (alk. paper)
Subjects: LCSH: Idealism. | Pluralism.
Classification: LCC B823 .A83 2017 | DDC 141—dc23
LC record available at https://lccn.loc.gov/2017006995

for my students,
idealizers and idealists

Contents

Preface

Truth is the shattered mirror strown
In myriad bits; while each believes his little bit the
whole to own.

SIR RICHARD BURTON,
The Kasîdah of Hâjî Abdû El Yezdî

This book grew out of a series of lectures whose central claim was that, as the German philosopher Hans Vaihinger argued about a century ago, questions about idealization are of central importance in all the major areas of philosophy. The lectures were meant to stimulate more people to consider these questions over a wider range—a wider range, in fact, than any one person could responsibly cover. But often in philosophy it is useful to stand back and take a broad view of a topic, knowing that real progress requires work with a narrower focus as well.

I offer this book in that spirit, hoping that it will prove useful in encouraging further explorations of idealization in aesthetics, ethics, and metaphysics, as well as in the philosophy of mind, of language, of religion, and of the social and natural sciences. And that further work, I want to persuade you, will profit from seeing the connections among these many fields.

My aim, then, is not so much to announce any startling discoveries as to persuade you that idealization matters in all the major areas of the humanities and the sciences and in everyday life, and to commend it as a topic of reflection and research. But there *is* a general lesson that I do want to underline at the start: Once we come to see that many of our best theories are idealizations, we will also see why our best chance of understanding the world must be to have a plurality of ways of thinking about it. This book is about why we need a multitude of pictures of the world. It is a gentle jeremiad against theoretical monism. There will, I hope, be other lessons along the way. But I am going to begin with Hans Vaihinger's neglected work, because he made the question of idealization central to his philosophy.

In Chapter 1, then, I introduce some of Vaihinger's ideas. We'll see how they might work out in the case of some familiar idealizations we make in thinking about human thought and behavior. At least since Aristotle, philosophers have tried to give accounts of why people do what they do by exploring the thoughts—the beliefs, desires, and the like—that would make their actions rational. But, also from way back, we've known that their actions *weren't* rational, or at least not fully so. The natural thing to say here is that we're idealizing. What does that mean?

In Chapter 2, I will explore in some detail a particular problem involving idealization and ideals that should interest philosophers of psychology and the social sciences, which has to do with one way of thinking about probability. I will end with some observations about the relationship between idealization and fiction, which will show that we respond as if things were so not only cognitively but emotionally as well. And in Chapter 3, I will be considering the role of what John Rawls called "ideal" and "non-ideal" theory in thinking about political philosophy, trying to distinguish various objections to the way he conceived of the task of political philosophy. There I shall argue that in moral and political philosophy, there is a role for a great variety of different idealizing assumptions about the same subject matter.

To say that it is good often to proceed by way of idealization is to argue that sometimes, in thinking about the world, truth isn't what you need. For, as Vaihinger argued, an idealization is a useful untruth. Insisting upon this point runs against a disciplinary habit of mind. Philosophers have a soft spot for truths. Indeed, it is an affection I share. And yet hardly anything we ordinarily say is clearly true.

Take just the last three sentences, by way of example. The first is what linguists call a generic, like "Tigers eat people." There are notorious difficulties with generics.[1] Who are the relevant philosophers? How many of them must have this soft spot? What exactly makes sentences of the form "X has a soft spot for Y" true, anyway? The second sentence inherits all these difficulties: What "affection" is articulated in the first sentence? As for the third sentence, what makes it true that "hardly any Xs are Ys"? How many or what proportion of the things philosophers say must fail to be clearly true? What, for that matter, is it to be—or not to be—clearly true?

You will no doubt have your own answers to these questions. Still, we can agree that each of those sentences is in some way factually defective—merely truthy, in a recent satiric idiom, rather than true— but not much the worse for that. And trying to say something interesting on almost any topic that isn't open to similar objections will show you how hard it is to get away from this sort of routine defection from the truth.

There are many other reasons for doubting that truth is always the point of assertion. Among the most obvious of them is the pervasiveness of figurative language, which (to use a figure) shows its untruthfulness on its face. When, to cite a familiar example, Romeo announces that "Juliet is the sun," and that "yonder window" is the east, what he is saying is so obviously untrue that we must interpret his utterance as aimed at communicating a thought that it does not literally express. When Wordsworth speaks of the daffodils in his beloved Lake District as

> Continuous as the stars that shine
> And twinkle on the milky way . . .

we grasp that we are not meant to believe (or even to believe that the poet believes) that those thousands of flowers flow on across the shores of Grasmere on precisely the same scale as the billions of stars, visible and invisible, in our galaxy. As with Shakespeare's metaphor and Wordsworth's hyperbole, so too with synecdoche, litotes, and a score of other figures: what matters to us is not the truth asserted but some idea or feeling suggested or implied. (Often, naturally, it does matter whether some implicated thought is true.) These figures are literary; and much of literature—though, notice, not "Daffodils"—consists of fictions, which are not even offered up as true.

In these pages I aim, as I say, to explore some truth-related inadequacies that are different from these—not literary fiction, not figurative language—but, I hope, at least as interesting. At the end I'll return briefly to the question why so many of the things we say, in philosophy and the humanities and the sciences as in ordinary life, are instructive, even though not true. I shall argue that it isn't because truth is unimportant. In fact, I shall try to persuade you that if we didn't understand truth, we wouldn't be able to understand these half-truths either.

Some readers will notice that, in the standard way, I proceed as if one can sort out epistemic ideals from moral and political ones. With many of our everyday concepts, I grant, doing so can be enormously difficult. But some thoughtful philosophers doubt that moral and metaphysical or epistemological presuppositions can be disentangled even in principle.[2] So let me acknowledge that I am, in a certain sense, a Humean: I think there is always a distinction to be made between how things are and how they ought to be. (Or, as Hume put it in the *Treatise*, the move from "is" to "ought" is "of the last consequence.")[3] Nietzsche rightly mocked the notion that the "*consensus sapientium* establishes the truth," and yet there is something to be said for starting with the current consensus, even if we don't end there.[4]

It will be worth explicitly distinguishing one other set of questions that I am not going to be exploring. Some philosophers think there are domains where all the things we say are a form of fictional talk. Some take morality, in particular, to be such a domain, saying that moral claims do not represent the world at all, but are, in some way, expressions of feelings or commitments, rather than of real beliefs. These philosophers are willing to use the word "true," but only as a way of saying that they share the feelings or commitments that another person has expressed in making a moral claim. I find this view intelligible (even tempting) but I do not share it. Other philosophers think that there are, strictly speaking, no truths at all—about anything. This I find harder to understand. But for the purposes of this book I don't need to address views like these. Claims of this sort about a whole domain are, I will say, metaphysical: they involve giving up the contrast between a thought's being true and our being entitled to treat it, in certain respects, as if it were true. I am interested, on the other hand, in cases where we (believe we) have a grip on the notion of truth and yet we have reason to go on using a theory that is, in some way or other, for some reason or another, not true.[5] So I take the notion of truth for granted, without relying on an answer to the question how it should be understood metaphysically for each class of theories I'm discussing. Even though the metaphysical questions strike me as interesting and important, I think they are dissimilar and respond to different arguments. In the end, I hope to encourage both those who are averse to any recourse to useful fictions and those disinclined to distinguish useful fictions from truths to consider an approach in which fiction and fact each play indispensable roles.

As If

I

Useful Untruths

Lessons from Hans Vaihinger

But object, attribute, and the judgment in which
they are combined, are fictions, i.e., errors—but
fruitful errors.

HANS VAIHINGER,
The Philosophy of "As If"

The Philosophy of "As If"

Imagine that you were raised in a devout Swabian
parsonage near Tübingen in the mid-nineteenth
century and grew up with great respect for the
leading theologians of your age. Imagine, too, that
you had the profoundest engagement with the ethical and aesthetic dimensions of Christianity. Suppose, finally, that you became a serious student of
Kant, Schopenhauer, and Nietzsche, and that you
moved, in part as a result, from theism to pantheism

to agnosticism, while still retaining your Christian ethical and aesthetic commitments. Because, like all educated men and women of your place and time, you were familiar with classical Greek and Roman ideas, you might have come to feel that, "according to the custom of the cultured Greeks and Romans, . . . one may regard and treat these myths as 'myths' and yet (or rather just because of this) continue to esteem such fictions for their ethical and aesthetic value."[1] That was pretty much what happened to Hans Vaihinger, the philosopher who wrote these words in the autobiographical essay that prefaced his 1911 magnum opus *Die Philosophie des Als Ob*, translated in 1924 into English by C. K. Ogden as *The Philosophy of "As If."*

Vaihinger tells us he had reached the view that theology was composed of "myths" by his midtwenties, about the time of his graduation from Tübingen University. Over the next forty years—as the founding editor of *Kantstudien* (1896) and of *Annalen der Philosophie* (1919) (which was to be taken over by Rudolf Carnap and Hans Reichenbach and reborn as *Erkenntnis*), and as a student of the history of mathematics and the physical sciences and the psychology of his day—Vaihinger came to apply the same strategy over and over again to one field after another, abandoning realism about a domain (atoms, infinitesimals, law, space, abstract objects, force, economics, freedom) but maintaining his "esteem" for the corresponding ideas because of their utility.[2] And, in explicitly connecting this strategy with the one that Kant had made famous in arguing that rational agency requires us to act *as if* we were free, even though our theoretical understanding shows that we are governed by deterministic laws, he claimed a Kantian ancestry for his ideas. Indeed, in the final section of *The Philosophy of "As If,"* Vaihinger records scores of places in Kant's work where his great predecessor speaks of proceeding "as if" what is theoretically known to be false is true.[3] (He goes on, by the way, to do the same thing for Nietzsche.)

Vaihinger's suggestion that large areas of our thought are fictions amounts to this: Very often we can reasonably proceed as if what we know to be false is true *because it is useful for some purpose to do so.* In the present moment, when too many seem inclined to speak untruth because it is politically useful to do so, I anticipate that some will worry that Vaihinger risks providing here a high-minded philosophical defense of what is, in fact, a low-minded political practice. So, let me briskly mark some of the ways in which our unhappy proliferation of "alternative facts" is not what Vaihinger had in mind. The fundamental point is that Vaihinger is interested in the role of untruth in *thinking* about reality, not in the usefulness of *speaking* untruths. He is engaged, to use an old distinction, in a logical rather than a rhetorical exploration. He is interested, therefore, in cases where the user of the fiction is aware, or can be made aware, that what she is thinking is not true. None of his cases involve deception or even the intention to deceive; he has no interest in defending expedient political lies. On the contrary, Vaihinger's formulation in terms of the idea that a thought might be useful for some purpose other than mirroring reality invites us to consider what that purpose is . . . and whether it is good or evil.

There are shades in Vaihinger's view of the sort of pragmatism that William James was talking about when he said, "Whenever a dispute is serious, we ought to be able to show some practical difference that must follow from one side or the other's being right."[4] Or when Charles Sanders Peirce before him said, "The essence of a belief is the establishment of a habit; and different beliefs are distinguished by the different modes of action to which they give rise."[5]

This view of beliefs as fundamentally serving their function in action is evident on the very first page of Vaihinger's "General Introductory Remarks on Fictional Constructs": "It must be remembered that the object of the world of ideas as a whole is not the portrayal of reality—this would be an utterly impossible task—but rather to provide an *instrument for finding our way about more easily in the world.*"[6] Vaihinger proposed, in essence, that an idealization is a useful untruth, a falsehood nevertheless useful for "finding our way about." As he once put it, fictions are "errors—but fruitful errors." And for anyone interested in this powerful way of thinking about idealization, Vaihinger's work is a trove of interesting resources.

Vaihinger obviously differs from at least one strand of pragmatism. He thinks that there is a gap between what is true and what it is useful to believe. That's why he asserts that most of our thought is best understood as fiction. If you equated the true and the useful to believe—as pragmatists are sometimes said to do—you would lose exactly the contrast that guided *The Philosophy of "As If."* And that book is the work of the modern philosopher who thought longest and hardest about this particular tangle of ideas, and certainly thought about its application over the widest range. Others may have gone deeper into idealization in one sphere or another; but Vaihinger is the thinker who first defined clearly the issues I aim to come to grips with.

Real Fictions and Semi-fictions

Vaihinger's notion of what he called a "real fiction" is in one way quite surprising. A real fiction, he held, involved a thought that was not just false but contradictory—in the sense in which he thought such useful ideas as the square root of a negative number in mathematics, or the atom in physics and chemistry, were contradictory. On his view, when we understand the world as composed of atoms— remember we are in the physics and chemistry of the late nineteenth century—we are supposing something that we know to be not just false but impossible. Suppose, "following Cauchy, Ampère, Seguin and Moigno, we designate the atoms as centres without extension": the result "turns out to be a very strange construction indeed. For an entity without extension that is at the same time a substantial bearer of forces—that is simply a combination of words with which no definite meaning can be connected."[7] Conceiving an atom as a point mass seems to require, among other things, that it should be infinitely dense. What sense, Vaihinger invites us to ask, can one make of that? And what sense could we make of the imaginary number, which Gauss had put to such good use in the early nineteenth century? Vaihinger insisted, in one of his characteristic paradoxes, "The concept in question is contradictory, but necessary."[8]

Vaihinger contrasted these *real* fictions with what he called "semi-fictions," where the "concepts only contradict reality as given, or deviate from it, but are not in themselves contradictory."[9] He gives as an expository example of a semi-fiction the Linnean system of classification, whose categorization of organisms is artificial because it does not reflect the real "natural" system of classification, which is one that "corresponds with reality in every respect."[10] Vaihinger's idea is that the Linnean classification is a fiction because we know there is nothing in the world that corresponds to it. That strikes me as a mistake. Provided that a system of classification assigns every object in its domain to just one category, the claim that an individual is a member of some class, however uninteresting, is surely true. The problem with the Linnean system is not that it is a useful falsehood, but that it is an unexplanatory truth: we do not know *why* the creatures in Linnae-us's species belong together. Only after Darwin do we have the possibility of systematic classification guided by a plausible theory.

A better example (which Vaihinger also offers) might be Adam Smith's assumption that people are rational egoists, seeking to maximize their own advantage. Vaihinger understands this assumption as one that Smith knew to be false, but that neverthe-less allowed the Scottish philosopher to construct a useful predictive economics. "The empirical mani-festations of human actions," Vaihinger wrote,

> are so excessively complicated that they present al-most insuperable obstacles when we try to under-stand them theoretically and reduce them to causal factors. For the construction of his system of political economy it was essential for Adam Smith to interpret human activity causally. With unerring instinct he realized that the main cause lay in egoism and he formulated his assumption in such a way that all human actions, and particu-larly those of a business or politico-economical nature, could be looked upon *as if* their driving force lay in one factor—egoism. Thus all the sub-sidiary causes and partially conditional factors,

such as good will, habit and so forth, are here neglected. With the aid of this abstract cause Adam Smith succeeded in bringing the whole of political economy into an ordered system.[11]

Nevertheless, Vaihinger argued, these "provisional assumptions . . . are, or at least should be, accompanied by the consciousness that they do not correspond to reality and that they *deliberately substitute a fraction of reality for the complete range of causes and effects.*"[12] Adam Smith's theory is a semi-fiction because it offers an account of the world that begins with an assumption—humans are rational egoists—which its proponent and those to whom he commends it all know to be untrue.

Beyond the distinction between "real fictions" and "semi-fictions," Vaihinger offered a complex taxonomy of the larger category to which they both belonged, "scientific fictions." Linnaeus illustrated "artificial classification," as we saw. Smith illustrated what he called "abstractive (neglective) fictions," as did such "average fictions" as Quetelet's *l'homme moyen.* There were "schematic" fictions, including what "might also be called the fiction of *the simple case.*" There were analogical fictions, juristic fictions, summational fictions, and, significantly, "heuristic fictions," which were often "former hypotheses which render services to science even in their present emaciated condition."[13] Of all these many distinctions, the one between fictions and hypotheses is the most uncontroversially helpful. Vaihinger's point was that the very same claim—men are rational egoists, say, in Adam Smith—could be treated as either a fiction (that is, a useful untruth) or as something whose actual truth remains an open possibility. And a good deal of his argument amounts to saying that many theories that are offered as hypotheses need not be given up when some of their claims are known to be false, because we can continue with them, treating them now as fictions.

These days, a distinction is often drawn between so-called Galilean and Aristotelian idealizations—between introducing distorting simplifications (planes without friction; agents with perfect information), on the one hand, and stripping out complications that are deemed to be negligible for the purposes at hand, on the other; between idealizing by abstraction and idealizing by approximation.[14] Of course, the line between approximation and omission is far from bright, and it's not always easy to say when a complicating factor has been stripped out through abstraction and when it has just been assumed to be too small to make a practical difference. Does the Wright-Fischer model of genetic drift cross over from an abstraction to an approximation when it makes its many counterfactual assumptions explicit? Vaihinger was inclined to think that the "method of approximation" (where an abstract solution is posited and then gradually brought toward reality by experimental correction) was "in principle . . . not different from the neglective one."[15]

Contradictory Assumptions

The difficulty posed by Vaihinger's emphasis on the contradictory fiction—on a model that is internally inconsistent—is obvious: How can an idealization be *useful*, given that (as we teach our students in introductory logic) if a theory is inconsistent, we can deduce from it anything at all? A "prediction" that something will happen *and* that it won't happen is not really a prediction.

As any logician will tell you, one can indeed construct so-called paraconsistent logics of which the general thesis that "from a contradiction anything follows" is false. But the status of these ideas is mired in controversy. And surely the way we corral the many actual inconsistencies in our thought is not by the implementation of a nonstandard logic but by what you might call functional isolation; so that, in effect, we have a large set of families of beliefs, each of which we try to keep consistent, and these families are not usually brought together in deliberation.[16]

The philosopher David Lewis once exemplified this sort of thing in a nice story about how he failed for a while to notice that for some purposes he acted as if a certain street in Princeton were parallel to the railway track, and for other purposes as if it were at right angles to it: everybody has experiences of the inconsistency of such "internal maps."[17] This isn't so different from the working chemist who switches between VB and MO—valence-bonding and molecular-orbital—theories of the chemical bond, two strictly incompatible models that arose at the same time and have shared a room, if not a bed, ever since. This sort of functional isolation, using incompatible theories for distinct purposes, is one I will return to more than once in the pages ahead.

In other instances, though, we might want to bring together theories with contradictory assumptions. In a widely discussed paper, Richard Levins, writing as both a practitioner and a theorist, elaborated on the multiplicity of models in population biology, and suggested that combining them can help us see whether our results flow from the details of the "simplifying assumptions" or from the "essentials" of the model.[18] An inference common to different models is, he said, more likely to be "robust."

It has often been remarked, certainly, that scientific explanations in contemporary physics involve mathematically inconsistent theories—or, to speak more carefully, involve the application at the same time of models that are inconsistent with each other, even if each of them is itself consistent. Using these theories involves, in effect, knowing which lines of inference one should and which one should not follow. Nancy Cartwright, for example, has criticized what she calls the "vending-machine" model of scientific theories, in which "you feed in certain prescribed forms for the desired output; it gurgitates for a while; then it drops out the sought-for representation, plonk, on the tray, fully formed, as Athena from the brain of Zeus."[19] Rather, she argues, using theories involves knowing how to take advantage of the available formal resources to treat specific phenomena. The argument lends texture to Vaihinger's idea that our idealizations are often contradictory. But that's because the understanding of the world implicit in the scientific theory—the knowledge it delivers—is held not just in the abstract statement of it but in the skill of applying it to certain standard cases: in particular, to what Cartwright calls "nomological machines," where a nomological machine is "a fixed (enough) arrangement of components, or factors, with stable (enough) capacities that in the right sort of stable (enough) environment will, with repeated operation, give rise to the kind of regular behaviour that we represent in our scientific laws."[20] A nomological machine—like the solar system, which she gives as one example—is screened off enough from outside forces that we can make roughly reliable laws about its motions (or other aspects of its behavior). So the physicist's knowledge is held not just in the formal theory but also in the understanding that one can use specific formal resources to treat particular kinds of situations: which is one reason why its inconsistency should worry us less.[21]

These considerations suggest that Vaihinger was right about something important. You can't refute the claim that our best theories are inconsistent by arguing that the world itself can't be inconsistent, unless you presuppose that our best theories aim only at truth. But the criteria we sensibly use in evaluating theories go beyond verisimilitude. That is already conceded once we allow for the idea that we can accept an idealizing theory; and, as Mathias Frisch put it not so long ago (apropos, as it happens, of classical electrodynamics), we need to allow for the possibility "that the representations of the phenomena in a certain domain that are most successful in balancing various theoretical virtues, such as those proposed by Kuhn, are mutually inconsistent" and that further research won't "lead to both more successful and jointly consistent representations."[22]

Vaihinger himself was influenced, as I say, not only by his reading of the physics of his day and the developments in the mathematical theory of imaginary numbers, but also by many other sorts of cases. He discusses the contradictions alleged against the treatment of infinities and infinitesimals in the differential calculus; he explores Kant's insistence, in the first *Critique*, that there were antinomies of reason, so that reason could lead us in each of two (apparently) contradictory directions. But although Vaihinger may have exaggerated the prevalence of the self-contradictory idealization, it's worth holding on to the idea that idealization may involve contradictory presuppositions. This arises even in the most basic case: If an idealization involves knowingly acting *for some purposes* as if what is false is true, then using it means that you are treating a proposition as true while, in another part of your head, so to speak, you are regarding it as false.[23] (It will always be important to remember that treating a thought as if it were true is treating it as if it were true for some purposes and some contexts. Why would one treat a thought as if it were true for *all* contexts and purposes unless one just believed it, *tout court*? I shall say more about this issue at the end of Chapter 2.)

Vaihinger's talk of contradictions fends off one strategy for defending idealizations, which is to suppose that an idealized model describes precisely what would have happened in certain counterfactual circumstances where the idealizing assumptions were true. For even though there are various heroic attempts to defend the notion that one can make sense of counterfactuals whose antecedents are logically impossible, these counterfactuals are mostly unintelligible: we are not usually interested in what would be true in an (or the) impossible world.[24]

Notice that, once we grant that our models assume what is not so, the fact that another proposition is inconsistent with a model we currently have cannot, by itself, count against accepting it.[25] For we know, *ex hypothesi*, that we already have a picture that is untrue to how things, strictly speaking, are. So the success of our current model, for some purpose or other, cannot count against accepting an additional model that is inconsistent with it, for at least two reasons. One is that just because our theory, which is not strictly true, succeeds to some degree for some purpose, we cannot infer that another theory inconsistent with it could not also succeed to more or less the same degree for the same purpose; the other is that what is successful for some purposes might not be successful for others. The result is that Vaihinger can give us an explanation for why we might profit from mobilizing a set of theories that are inconsistent with one another.[26]

Useful for What?

But if idealization is, as Vaihinger proposed, a matter of useful untruths, there are now two kinds of questions to ask that are familiar from discussions of pragmatist ideas about what it is useful to believe.

First, useful for what . . . and when? And second, if a falsehood is useful, isn't there some truth in the vicinity that would be even more useful? Why stick with the useful untruth? Won't the truth always be better? I'll return to this second line of questioning shortly. For the moment, though, let's stick with the first.

One old line of thought here—a thought almost as old as systematic philosophy itself—is that utility means usefulness in "saving the phenomena": A simplifying idealization is useful if it allows us to cover the past record and predict the future course of our experiences. A theory can be useful because it allows us to predict what will happen over a wide range of cases, even if we know that it is false. That is the situation with many of the laws of nineteenth-century physical chemistry. For example, the pressure law tells us that the pressure of a gas, held within a vessel, will rise as the temperature rises, increasing in proportion to the absolute temperature. This result can be derived by a theory in which pressure corresponds to the average force on the wall of the vessel caused by the impacts of gas molecules as a function of their mass and their velocity, and where temperature is a manifestation of the mean kinetic energy of the molecules. This is one of those places Vaihinger noticed where the assumption that gases consist of point masses—atoms with mass and velocity but no volume—can nevertheless allow us to predict an actual phenomenon. But the predictions here are only roughly right—as the molecules of the gas get bigger and more complex, for example, the relationship between pressure and temperature is far from linear. The pressure law is useful for some gases over a range of temperatures—and better over a wider range for gases composed of smaller molecules—because it gets the pressure–temperature relationship roughly right. It is natural enough, then, to suppose that Vaihinger meant that what these false theories could be useful for was prediction. But despite some passages that suggest this picture, this is not exactly Vaihinger's view.

In his introduction he says, "The test of the correctness of a logical result lies in *practice*, and the purpose of thought must be sought not in the reflection of a so-called objective world, but in rendering possible the calculation of events and of operations upon them." The "purpose of thought," then, is, he says, "to keep us constantly in a position to deal with things so that, with given conditions, relations, stipulations, and circumstances, we may receive an exactly ascertainable sense-impression (for every determination of objective data ultimately rests on that, and can be established in no other way); and so that, by such and such an impulse under such conditions, we may produce an exactly ascertainable effect, which in its turn cannot be observed except by means of certain sensations."[27]

The point, as a result, is that it is in *controlling* the world that "thought" proves itself useful; and even though "sensation" is our only means of access to the world, the object of "thought" is not to manufacture predictions about our sensations but to control the world. There are philosophers who think that, because all we know about the world is how it seems to us, there is no difference between aiming at shaping how things seem and aiming at shaping how things are. This claim belongs to the world of metaphysical views that I said at the start I was going to avoid. For it is associated with the idea that, in the domain of theories about the physical world, there is no point to the distinction between being really true and merely seeming to be true. Bas van Fraassen, for example, endorses a view that he calls constructive empiricism, which holds that "science aims to give us theories which are empirically adequate; and acceptance of a theory involves a belief only that it is empirically adequate." And a theory "is empirically adequate," in his account, "exactly if what it says about the observable things and events in the world is true—exactly if it 'saves the phenomena.'"[28]

On this view, it doesn't matter whether the things that a scientific theory says about unobservables— electrons, say—are true or false. But what Vaihinger was interested in was the case where the distinction between the true and the false does matter . . . *and we have a justification for sticking with the false.* People sometimes object to van Fraassen's position by insisting that it would be a miracle if a theory were empirically adequate but not true. This is not, I think, an interesting question about any current theory, given that no interesting current theory is fully empirically adequate. (I am confident no general physical theory will ever be completely empirically adequate, for reasons that will be clear, I hope, by the end of Chapter 2.) The mystery I am interested in is not the miracle alleged against van Fraassen: it is a puzzle about why a theory that is not even empirically adequate can nevertheless be a useful thing to hang on to.

In believing that something is so, I find myself disposed to act in a certain way. If all the beliefs on which I act are true, the things I try to do will happen—I will control what I aim to control. In believing that it is *as if* something is so, I dispose myself to act in a certain way, but only in certain contexts and for certain purposes. In that context and for those purposes I will do what I would have done if I had just straight out believed it. As a result, I have reasons to act as if something were so— as I would if I believed it to be so *tout court*—in a certain context if I have reason to think that, in *that* context, my acts are likely to succeed if I do so.

Vaihinger's treatment has the great virtue that it regards questions concerning our everyday thinking about the world as continuous with our scientific thinking: Both aim, he says, at controlling reality, and both can leave things out in order to make it practicable to represent the world we want to control.[29] Notice that Vaihinger does not say that beliefs about Xs have it as their function to control Xs. That was a wise choice. One thing a belief about X can entail is that there is nothing a person can do to change the state of X: that is true of my beliefs about black holes and supernovas. But equipped with those beliefs (and a whole host of others) I can control telescopes in ways that produce results that depend on the condition of these large astronomical objects.[30] Control is critical, then, to what he breezily called *"finding our way about more easily in the world."*

So Vaihinger believed that our thoughts are tools that allow us to control (some features of) the world. But why, according to him, must we embrace what we know to be false? Let's begin by examining a passage Vaihinger refers to in Henry Thomas Buckle's *Introduction to the History of Civilization in England*, where the nineteenth-century historian discusses Adam Smith's idealizations. "Adam Smith, in his *Wealth of Nations*," Buckle had written, "simplified the study of human nature by curtailing it of all its sympathy." "But," he continued, "this most comprehensive thinker was careful, in his *Theory of the Moral Sentiments*, to restore to human nature the quality of which the *Wealth of Nations* had deprived it; and by thus establishing two different lines of argument, he embraced the whole subject."[31] Buckle is overreaching here, of course. For the *complete* treatment would presumably include not just egoism and sympathy but *all* the psychological factors relevant for explaining human behavior. And, as is suggested by a passage I cited earlier, one of Vaihinger's thoughts is that it is precisely the difficulty of embracing "the whole subject" that makes idealization inescapable. It's the fact that the phenomena are "excessively complicated" that requires us to leave out some of the details.

But to say that the complexity is *excessive* is to make a point not so much about the world as about our understanding of it: The complexities exceed *our* cognitive capacity to encompass *them*, and that is as much a fact about *us* as about *them*.[32] Suppose, for example, that the quantum theory were precisely true. In principle, I guess, that would allow us to write a precise equation for each of the atoms in a baseball. To describe the baseball, we would then have to solve a system of the order of at least 10^{24} equations. No human being knows how to do this mathematics; no human-made machine could do it either. And even if there were such a machine, what understanding would it deliver to you and me? It has become a familiar thought that our idealizations may reflect the need for a trade-off between accuracy and ease, precision and computational tractability.[33]

If the utility of scientific fictions derives from the excessive complexity of the world—that is, from the fact that its complexity exceeds *our* cognitive capacities—the utility of religious myth seems to

derive from elsewhere. Vaihinger pronounces himself here a disciple of Friedrich Albert Lange, whose
History of Materialism articulated a "standpoint of
the ideal" that permits a metaphysical atheist to
hold on to religion as myth because of what he
calls the "ethical efficacy" of religious language.[34]
Vaihinger did not deny that atheists could have
moral convictions—he did not think that if God is
dead, everything is permitted. But he *did* think
that we are more likely to be able to live by our
ideals if we express them—"poetically," as it were—
in religious language. ("All the nobler aspects of
life are based upon fictions," he wrote.[35] As we've
seen, he thought the ignobler aspects were based
on fictions, too.)

This is meant, I think, as an empirical claim; I
shall not canvass the evidence for or against it here.
Richard Braithwaite, one of my earliest teachers in
philosophy (and the person whose poker Ludwig
Wittgenstein is supposed to have flourished in the
general direction of Karl Popper during their con-
frontation at a Moral Sciences Club meeting) argued
later—in his Eddington lecture "An Empiricist's
View of the Nature of Religious Belief"—that one
could understand and adopt religious beliefs without
an appeal to theology; in effect, then, he thought

one could treat the creed he recited on Sundays explicitly as fiction.[36] And Vaihinger's strategy of argument shows that the utility of fictions can be seen not just in their power to aid us in manipulating the world outside us but also in their capacity to help us manage our selves. His thought, like Kant's thought about the inevitability of the idea of freedom in the world of the understanding, is that we can grasp theoretically that the ideas we are using are false, while still finding them practically useful . . . indeed inescapable.

So, suppose, with Vaihinger, that *useful* means "useful for managing the world, including, sometimes, ourselves." Then there's a puzzle about how we can make good predictions by, for example, leaving stuff out. Vaihinger's answer here, I think, can be twofold: First, sometimes leaving stuff out makes too little difference to matter for the purpose at hand, as when, in a commonly cited example, we use Newtonian rather than Einsteinian mechanics in our bridge building. But Vaihinger also has a second answer. Sometimes our idealizations allow us to get things right because we proceed, as it were, in two steps—first, by ignoring a range of phenomena in order to build a model of a world without them, and then, once we have grasped how that model works, by adding more and more of the world gradually back in. As he put it:

> If, in fictions, thought contradicts reality, or if it even contradicts itself, and if in spite of this questionable procedure it *nevertheless* succeeds in corresponding to reality, then—and this is a necessary inference—*this deviation must have been corrected and the contradiction must have been made good.*[37]

Now Vaihinger was, in the end, something of an instrumentalist about theory. He focused, as we have seen, on the role of our theories in controlling the world. The function of theoretical language, in his view, was to help us *do* something, first of all; it was an instrument for managing reality, not a mirror held up to the world. (I am not endorsing this contrast: a mirror can be an instrument for managing reality.) The line of thinking adumbrated here might suggest another use of idealization, in which we take the role of the idealized model as helping us not so much to predict or control the world as to *understand* it. Which of these is our aim will make a difference to what models are useful.

Consider an effort, seven decades back, to explain how the brain gives rise to the mind. The stakes were explanatory, but they did not feel small.

"For the first time in the history of science, we know how we know," one of its principals told a university philosophy club in a lecture titled "In the Den of the Metaphysician."[38]

Molecules of Thought

The paper that distilled the effort, "A Logical Calculus of the Ideas Immanent in Nervous Activity," came out in 1943, and represented an intensive collaboration between Warren S. McCulloch (1898–1968) and Walter Pitts (1923–1969). Both had been much taken by Russell and Whitehead's *Principia Mathematica* (an encounter that, for Pitts, came at age twelve) and later by Alan Turing's famous 1936 paper on computability. The result is what has been credited as the first computational theory of the brain.[39] McCulloch had long worked in neurophysiology and was then at the Neuropsychiatric Institute of the University of Illinois Medical Center in Chicago; the precocious Walter Pitts, a student of Carnap's, brought a rigorous armamentarium of mathematical and logical methods. They were after a sort of proof of principle. Recognizing that "the nervous system is a net of neurons," they wanted to suggest how interlinked neurons might be able to give rise to thought by showing how they could encode logical functions.

They spelled out their premises. To fire, they stipulated, a neuron must receive some fixed number of exciting impulses, within "the period of latent addition" (less than a quarter of a millisecond), a number that would put it over the neuron's fixed firing threshold, a value that they designated θ. But the neuron won't fire if it receives a single *inhibiting* impulse. (Inhibition would be assigned a negative value and a weight that guaranteed it would trump a full array of positive inputs.) They also assumed that "the structure of the net does not change with time."[40]

McCulloch and Pitts saw that the "all or nothing" property of a neuron—it was either firing or not firing—was congruent with the true-false Boolean binary; all that remained was to demonstrate that a network of neurons, once they were mathematically idealized along these lines, could model the logical structure of propositions. Each input $(i_1, i_2, \ldots, i_n)$ is assigned a fixed weight, w_i, to represent the strength of its effect on the neuron, and, unlike the inputs, those weights can be given fractional values. (In reality, there are neurons with as many as a hundred thousand synaptic inputs, or "fan-ins"; giving integral weights for the values in such cases would be very cumbersome.) A McCulloch-Pitts neuron is defined by those fixed values; what varies are those one-or-zero impulses. If the sum of the weighted impulses $(w_1 i_1 + w_2 i_2 + \ldots)$ is equal to or greater than the threshold, θ, then, perhaps a millisecond later, the neuron fires (output of 1). If not, the output is a 0. In short, we had a function where a series of ones and zeros is the input and a series of ones and zeros is the output—a function, to be precise, that equals 0 unless

$$\sum_{i=1}^{n} i_i w_i \geq \theta$$

Set the right weights and threshold values, and you've got yourself an OR function: that is, an input of 1 and 0, or of 0 and 1, or of 1 and 1, will yield 1, in a way that corresponds to the standard truth tables for "or" in sentential logic. What might such a neuron look like? Suppose it's a two-input neuron, where w_1 is 2 and w_2 is 2, and θ is 2. Then, for the ordered pair of inputs (1, 1), our neuron is presented with $2 \times 1 + 2 \times 1$, which is greater than the threshold value of 2, and so its output is 1. Apply the weights to all the possible inputs—(1, 1), (1, 0), (0, 1), (0, 0)—and the respective outputs correspond to the result of an OR table: 1, 1, 1, 0, which is to say, T, T, T, F. To get an AND NOT neuron, where our two-input neuron fires only when presented with the ordered pair (1, 0), you could set the threshold at 2, w_1 at 2, and w_2 at −1.

By itself, a two-input McCulloch-Pitts neuron can't produce the XOR function, the exclusive disjunction operator, which yields true (1) when two inputs differ (true, false; false, true; or, equivalently, 1, 0; 0, 1). It can't model any function that's not linearly separable. But put two of them together, and they can model any binary Boolean function you please. With three, you can divide by two. You can even get memory, of a sort, because time is built into the system (each activation cycle represents some segment of time, enabling "delay gates") and because the output of one cell is input to another cell, which might provide input to the first cell, producing a feedback loop.

Although the picture was meant to show that neural nets constituted a Turing machine, the examples McCulloch and Pitts offered could be very homely. They could explain the "heat illusion" (hold an ice cube to your skin, remove it after a brief moment, and you'll experience a sensation of heat). They knew that there were cutaneous cold receptors and heat receptors. Consider, they said, a rule like this: The heat sensation neuron fires if the heat-reception neuron fires or if the cold-reception neuron fires once and ceases to fire. At other moments, the paper was wilder in its ambitions. The psychiatrist was to conclude that "in prognosis, history is never necessary," and come to believe that "diseased mentality can be understood, without loss of scope or rigor, in the scientific terms of neurophysiology."[41]

As it turned out, the influence of the paper was really greatest in the development of the modern computer—Von Neumann's "Report" on the EDVAC, laying out the architecture of the modern computer, cited no publication save the McCulloch-Pitts paper—and, even more, in research into artificial intelligence.[42] The beauty of the model was its simplicity, although soon this was felt to be *too* simple, and the severe idealization was complicated a bit. A big step was the introduction, in the late 1950s, of Frank Rosenblatt's perceptron, which added to the function another input, the bias, and allowed weights to be adjusted in response to the function's success or failure. The aim was to enable learning, via Hebb's rule: If cell A repeatedly excites adjacent cell B, A will grow more effective in exciting B.[43] The perceptron moved the idealized neural net from the chalkboard to the lab; the learning algorithm was actually put to use.

There is no doubt that these early models were useful for something. But it is hard to say exactly what. On the one hand, they offered, as I said earlier, a proof of principle: a system composed of elements that shared certain properties with neurons could carry out some of the logical functions the mindbrain must be able to perform. But it was always clear that actual neurons had properties very different from those of the McCulloch-Pitts neuron; and in any case, nobody then had any idea how to model in these terms something with 10^{11} neurons, each of which has an average of perhaps 10^4 links . . . something, that is, of the scale of a human brain.

Gradually the lure shifted from explaining human cognition to creating something that was, in certain respects, humanlike and neuromorphic but that didn't necessarily achieve these effects the way the brain did. What was conceived as an account, albeit highly abstracted, of how the brain's neuronal circuits could give rise to thought became, after repeated revision and augmentation, the schematic basis for research into artificial intelligence, into teaching machines how to think—or, at any rate, "think."

So a highly idealized model of the brain acquires independent utility because its simplifying idealizations ended up providing techniques for mimicking the functions rather than the material substrate of the mind. The McCulloch-Pitts neuron idealized radically the *structural* components of the nervous system and helped us understand how a brain composed of actual neurons might work. But our understanding of the mind could also proceed by way of an idealized model of the brain's *functions*, set free from assumptions about its constitution. We can see this idea worked out in the thought of the contemporary philosopher Daniel Dennett, whose work can be taken as a case study in Vaihinger's philosophy of the "as if." In thinking about his proposals, we can come to see the power of Vaihinger's picture in framing our understanding of idealization.

The Sorta True

I should say from the start that my object here is not to provide an interpretation of Dennett's work that he would accept. I am interested rather in exploring questions raised in his work that are central to my project of understanding idealization. This is a natural enough thing to do, given that Dennett has urged us to adopt what he calls "the intentional stance" toward many things (ourselves among them) and to adopt the "design stance," too, to many things (our selves included) as well. What we seem to have is about as straightforward an application of Vaihinger's idea as you could get—because to adopt the intentional stance toward a person is to treat her *as if* she were a rational agent with beliefs and desires—the beliefs and desires she "ought to have given [her] place in the world and [her] purpose"—and then to predict what this rational agent will do in order to further her goals. (The term "intentional" can be confusing, as Dennett cautions. In the usage established by Franz Brentano, intentionality means "aboutness"—the property of representing or "being about" something. The stance is *intentional*, then, because beliefs and desires are always *about* something, so you're supposing that people have states that are about things in the world.)[44] Similarly, to adopt the "design stance" toward organisms is to treat them *as if* they were designed to perform certain functions, and this can allow us to predict what they will do. Just as we explain what it is to be an intentional system by specifying the intentional stance, so we can say what it is to have a certain function by adopting the design stance—by treating something as if it had been made by a designer with certain aims.

In each case, adopting a stance of this sort involves treating something *as if* something were so: as if it had internal states of belief and desire, as if it were the product of purposive design. Again, it's the philosophy of "as if." I have been urging, with Vaihinger, that we do this a whole lot, in many domains. Dennett agrees.

But that leads once more to the question why it works (to allow predictions, in this case) when it does.[45] *If* it works, I've suggested, we have reasons to go along with it, even at the price of inconsistency: that is what Nancy Cartwright teaches us about much physics; it is what Vaihinger thought about theology, number theory, physics, and economics; and what Braithwaite thought about religious language. But showing *that* it does work doesn't explain *why*.

Dennett claims (at least some of the time) that beliefs and desires are real states of people: they are the states that, in fact, make it possible, when we adopt what he has dubbed "the intentional strategy," for us to predict what people will do. "To a first approximation," in his account, "the intentional strategy consists of treating the object whose behavior you want to predict as a rational agent with beliefs and desires and other mental states exhibiting what Brentano and others call *intentionality*." Doing so requires that you "figure out what beliefs and desires that agent ought to have, given its place in the world and its purpose." Then you predict that this rational agent will act to further its goals in the light of its beliefs and desires. The agent must be reasonable in two ways: first, it must form its beliefs and desires in ways that are reasonable; second, it must perform the acts that are reasonable given those beliefs and desires. (We can call the first sort of rationality *theoretical* or *epistemic* and the second *practical*.) To adopt this strategy in dealing with someone or something is to adopt the intentional stance toward it. What it is, finally, to have beliefs and desires is to be an "*intentional system*, a system whose behavior is reliably and voluminously predictable via the intentional strategy."

Now, does it matter *why* the agent's behavior is predictable in this way? If I have beliefs and desires and am rational, the reason the intentional strategy of treating me as a rational agent works, when it does, is: that I am a rational agent with those beliefs and desires. It works because it treats me as what I am. If the intentional strategy works with something that *doesn't* both have beliefs and desires and behave rationally, on the other hand, the success of those "reliable and voluminous" predictions might seem to be a mystery.

Dennett serves up an example that is supposed to show you why the success of the intentional stance can, in fact, be quite unmysterious. Consider a computer chess program. And ask yourself how to predict what it will do. Reading the program—or, worse, looking at the transistors of the computer that is implementing it—isn't going to be much help. It would take you much too long to read and understand the program (at least if the program is any good!). A much better way to predict its moves is to ask yourself this question: What would a reasonable person who knows the rules and the aim of chess do when faced with this board? You'd figure the computer "knows how" to play chess, "wants" to win, and will act accordingly. You would, in short, adopt the intentional stance. You would do pretty much exactly what you would do if you were trying to predict the moves that a *person* would make.

The reason this will often work is obvious: the computer was *designed* to make the best move it can. The better the design, the more likely it is that the intentional strategy will work . . . though—and, again, obviously—if it is really well designed it will "see" more possibilities and opportunities than most of us mortals would, and so we will get our predictions wrong. Predicting many of the moves of IBM's Deep Blue (the program that beat Garry Kasparov in 1997) is possible only for the grandest of Grand Masters.

The scare quotes around "knows," "knows how," "wants," and "sees," in some of Dennett's writing about this topic, draw attention to the fact that most of us, in adopting the intentional stance toward a computer, take talk of its beliefs and desires to be figurative, not literal, a *façon de parler* where we are clear that our mode is a kind of fiction. With humans, on the other hand, we take it literally. (And also with many other animals. I think the sheep on our farm know that we'll feed them. They don't just "know" it.) Dennett tells us we should "simply postpone" the "question of what *really* has a mind."[46] Unfortunately, there are reasons to worry about whether *any* actual thing really has a mind—as opposed to something a bit like a mind—on his story.

Here's why. You and I are supposed to be intentional systems. Our behavior can be reliably predicted when viewed from the intentional stance. So we meet one of Dennett's criteria. But neither of us is, as we will be reminded regularly in these pages, fully rational. Indeed, that we are going to do *irrational* things is also voluminously predictable. So it remains a bit of a mystery why the intentional strategy succeeds with us on the occasions that it does.

Dennett does not, I think, stress sufficiently the fact that the strategy also *fails* a good deal. It fails in part because the sort of rationality in question is extremely demanding: it involves having all the beliefs and desires we ought to have and acting only as we ought to act, given them. And the evident fact that many people don't believe what they ought to—that Barack Obama was born in Hawaii, for example—or desire what they should (to abstain from smoking, say) is one reason the strategy is not guaranteed to succeed. If you have to be fully rational to have beliefs and desires, then I don't have beliefs and desires and neither (excuse me for saying this) do you.

Dennett has an answer to the question why the intentional strategy works as often as it does. He thinks we were designed by evolution to work this way. And unlike many naturalist philosophers, he thinks there is nothing wrong in speaking of organisms (or their parts) as designed by evolution to do things.[47] This makes sense to him because, as I said, he thinks that just as we can adopt the intentional stance toward people (and animals and computers), we can adopt the design stance toward organisms and the things they produce: We can treat them as if they were designed to perform certain functions, and this can allow us to predict (reliably and voluminously, once more) what they will do. Once you know what an alarm clock or a chainsaw is *for*, you know what it will do. So, too, for a kidney or a heart. Here again, Dennett does not think it helpful to distinguish between what was really designed (by a capital-D Designer—Bishop Paley's divine clockmaker) and what is "merely" predictable once we adopt the design stance.[48]

You might think that Dennett is operating within that pragmatist tradition according to which our theories are to be evaluated by what they enable us to do. If the intentional stance enables us to predict the behavior of a computer, why not just accept that *it* has beliefs and desires and reasons? But that is not what he actually says.

What he proposes, instead, is that in the cases where the intentional stance is a rewarding strategy, yielding a budget of useful predictions and allowing us to manipulate the world to our advantage, we should say, not that the thing has beliefs and desires, but that it "sorta" has them. Dennett's use of the cozy word "sorta"—he pokes fun at the style of analytic philosophy by dignifying it as "the 'sorta' operator"—is one of the most interesting ideas in his recent philosophical writings.

Dennett uses this "operator" in two crucial ways. First, to talk about anything to which we can productively apply the intentional stance: if the strategy works, the thing sorta believes or desires. Second, in the context of evolution, to talk about the relationship between species and their ancestors. "Before there were bacteria," he writes, "there were sorta bacteria, and before there were mammals, there were sorta mammals, and before there were dogs, there were sorta dogs, and so on."[49]

It's easy to see one way the two uses are connected. For among the things that sorta believed were some of our ancestors. Beliefs came into being gradually, through an evolutionary process, and there's no exact moment when, suddenly—Hey, presto!—full-fledged belief appeared, just as there's no exact moment when the first mammal was born. "There is no principled line," Dennett says, "above which true comprehension is to be found."[50]

Sweet Mystery of Life

Why, though, is idealization a good strategy here? To unpack this question a little, let's no longer postpone the question whether anything has any actual beliefs. Adopting the intentional stance involves applying a rather elaborate theory to predict behavior. You treat the putative agent as having beliefs and desires, ascribed to it by supposing it believes and desires what it is reasonable for it to believe and to desire. And then you predict that it will do what it would be reasonable to do, granted it has those internal states. A creature that always had the rationally required states and did the rationally required thing—let us call it a Cognitive Angel—would always respond as the intentional stance expects. Its states would be full-fledged beliefs and desires, no sorta about it. *But there are no Cognitive Angels.* In the actual world, then, every belief is a "belief"—a sorta belief—and every desire is a "desire."

We can get to this conclusion by another route. For Dennett what matters is the empirical adequacy

of our ascriptions of beliefs and desires. But unlike
van Fraassen, he does not think that there is a further question whether an empirically adequate account of my actions is true—the states ascribed to
me by an empirically adequate theory would just be
the states I have.

The trouble is that it is not entirely clear what
"empirical adequacy" means here. Would it be
enough to predict *what* I would do? Or must a theory
predict as well exactly *when* I would do it? If empirical adequacy involves both, then we should have
more resources to distinguish two theories each of
which correctly said what I would do in a particular
context. But in order to predict more precisely when
I would act, you would presumably want to appeal to
features of my underlying states beyond the ones assumed by the folk theory of rational agency. And the
trouble is that *those* properties will usually involve
deviation from ideal rationality, because we will
have to take account of the characteristics of the processes by which imperfect creatures, with imperfect
memories and capacities for calculation, actually
make up their minds. (This is an issue that I will
take up again in more detail in Chapter 2.)

On Dennett's picture, in other words, so far as I
can see, the intentional strategy cannot produce an

empirically adequate account. Which is another reason for thinking that, on his view, we do not really have beliefs and desires.

In sum, looked at this way, we can interpret the intentional strategy like this: The strategy of prediction—the strategy we use to make sense of the behavior of all the things we can usefully treat as intentional systems—is to apply an idealized model, knowing that, because it *is* idealized, it won't always get things right. To say that something sorta believes is to say that the idealized model works well enough for practical purposes, in ordinary circumstances, with that thing. If it worked perfectly, it would be just plain true that the thing believes; if it works badly enough, it's plain false. In between is a vaguely delineated world of the sorta true.

As I said earlier, I doubt Dennett would accept my picture of his proposal. (As Robert's Rules of Order rightly insist, there are no friendly amendments.) Still, looking at it this way helps us to see that the right answer to the question whether anything at all really has a mind can be: sorta. But being sorta true is not, alas, a way of being true—it is a special way of false. And though it's easy to see why a true story should make the right predictions, why should a false one?

At the heart of Dennett's evolutionary account is a claim he first made at least as far back as *Elbow Room* (1984), his book on freedom of the will: The world is full of "free-floating rationales," reasons creatures do what they do, even though they don't know that that is why they do them. Squirrels bury nuts, which they will be able to eat in the winter. They don't know this when they bury them. But still, that's the reason they do it—they "have purposes but they don't need to know them. The Need to Know principle reigns in the biosphere, and natural selection itself doesn't need to know what it is doing."[51]

Dennett thinks that evolution has endowed *us*, on the other hand, with the capacity not just to *have* but also to *know* our purposes. And a proper evolutionary account of how we came to be sorta agents will make it unmysterious that we respond to reason's demands. The explanation of why the intentional strategy works for us is, in essence, that the design stance shows us why we have come to be intentional systems—that it is *as if* we were designed to have intentional states. But the mystery of why we can be managed by an intentional systems approach is not explained by saying that it is *as if* we were designed to work intentionally. It would be explained only if we *were* designed to work intentionally. We have only replaced one mystery with another.

Impasses such as these lead people to say that the fact that we can be predicted and controlled through the intentional strategy shows that there is an underlying truth that the approach captures. Ian Hacking has suggested, similarly, that what gives us reason to be realist about things like positrons is just that we can manipulate them, intervening in the world on the basis of our beliefs about them. Once, famously, when he was discussing a physics experiment with a friend, he asked how you alter the charge on a niobium ball. "'Well, at that stage,' said my friend, 'we spray it with positrons to increase the charge or with electrons to decrease the charge.'" Hacking's response: "From that day forth I've been a scientific realist. *So far as I'm concerned, if you can spray them then they're real.*"[52] And notice that, like Vaihinger, his thought is not about saving the phenomena but managing the world.

Nancy Cartwright, as we've seen, thinks that the success of the strategies of physics gives us reason to believe in the capacities our physical laws adumbrate imprecisely. In the same way, we might ask what better foundation there could be than the successes of the intentional strategy for believing in intentional states. Well, wouldn't we have a better reason if the theory didn't get so much wrong, in particular if it didn't treat us as rational in ways we already know we are not? Cartwright's view suggests an answer here that comes with her realism about the underlying states that she thinks the laws of physics aim to map. The failures are a consequence of the fact that other forces are intervening to stop the underlying capacities from showing themselves. So there is the possibility of an analogous response here from Dennett: We really have beliefs and desires. They would work as in a Cognitive Angel if there were no other forces operating in our minds to get in the way. The idealization is Galilean: it is supposing—acting as if—there are no other forces.

On each trip, every train of explanation comes to its last stop. Unless you think the whole world is the working out of conceptual necessities, you will have to accept that there are some brute empirical truths. For the moment I am inclined to think that the fact that the intentional strategy works to the extent that it does is in that way brute. Evolution equipped us with the intentional strategy, no doubt, and it was built in, presumably, because it was adaptive. But it seems to me that it is not at all clear yet *why* it is adaptive, what features of it led to its selection. And the hypothesis that we *really* have states that are like beliefs and desires is only one candidate explanation. You cannot doubt that you have beliefs and desires; it is hard realistically to doubt that other people have them.[53] It could be false, though, even if you couldn't doubt it. *Pace* Descartes, what cannot be doubted need not be true. Idealization works here, then, for reasons we do not understand.

But there is, in any case, a reason to doubt whether the question I am asking is a fair one. You cannot seriously answer the question why our idealizations work (when they do) except from the point of view of a picture of the world that includes both us and our idealizations, a picture that is, in that way, more comprehensive and detailed than any theory that we currently have. But we cannot do *anything* from the point of a view of a theory we don't have. If that is right, this sort of idealization will only be clearly visible, as it were, in the rearview mirror.

Seeing this should lead us to revisit Vaihinger's explanation as to why idealization is necessary. The question whether the complexity-for-us of the world explains our need for idealization requires us to have a picture of our own relation to the world. If the only picture we have of the world and of ourselves is an idealized one, we have no totally true theory with which to answer this question. We can try to answer it with these useful false theories, but they will, *ex hypothesi*, represent the world as simpler than it is. So, once more, it will only be from the point of view of theories that are better than ours that the question can sensibly be asked.

We can look back to Newtonian physics, for example, and ask why it worked well enough, even though it ignored complexities we now recognize. And we can see (from where we stand now) that it would have been very difficult, with the tools, both experimental and theoretical, that they mobilized, for nineteenth-century physicists to represent these post-Newtonian complexities. Similarly, the question I am asking Dennett to answer here may make sense only as a question we will be able to ask later looking backward at our present selves: and only then because we will suppose that our later theories are better. If that is right, then here, as elsewhere, in Hegel's famous image, the owl of Minerva flies at dusk.[54] We get to see a theory's situation more clearly only once we have left it behind.

Beyond Instrumentalism

Dennett's part-time instrumentalism gives the intentional stance a particular rationale. But as he would be the first to admit, this way of thinking of people is not recent; nor was it invented by a philosopher. Thinking of other people as having beliefs and desires is just the standard strategy of what we now call folk psychology, the way we all spontaneously think about how our minds work, at least if we have reached a certain age (about four) and we are not autistic.[55] It is not possible for human purposes to proceed with one another in any other way, and although you might entertain (as I already have) the possibility that this strategy presupposes a story that is not literally true, that will not lead you to abandon it. Paul Churchland may say that a scientific understanding of the mind will leave us without beliefs and desires, hopes, fears, and the like, but in ordinary life he won't refuse to answer questions about what he believes or hopes for.[56] And if he did, he couldn't interact with the rest of us in the ordinary ways that make everyday life possible. I am not offering this thought with the aim of refuting his eliminative materialism. Indeed, I have conceded that he may be right. But there is a sense in which it's beside the point to ask whether folk psychology is right or wrong. We are stuck using it because, in ways we may one day better understand, it is built into most of us. A functionalist idealization based in our everyday ways of making sense of each other is essentially irresistible; and there's a contrast here with the structural idealizations underlying the idea of the M-P neuron, which we could certainly do without. The texture of our experience, the way things spontaneously seem to us, our ability to co-ordinate with one another in everything from shopping to committing to a married life together—none of these would be possible in anything like their current form without thought and talk about belief and desire and a host of other propositional attitudes. If, as I have suggested, our folk psychology involves idealizations of our capacities for recall or for reason, these idealizations are constitutive of our mental and social lives. You can be a metaphysical eliminativist, like the Churchlands, about belief and still doubt that we can eliminate *talk* and *thought* about beliefs. ("Thought" here, presumably, will be what happens when we are talking to ourselves.) There is no place for us humans to stand and ask whether we really have the minds we think we have. Even as the light fades, we will be stuck looking out on the world with the intentional stance. A creature that did not do that would not have a human consciousness and could not take part in a human society.

Dennett may have exaggerated the extent to which understanding people makes them predictable. But when I meet you at the movie theater after a quick conversation on the phone, my expectation that you would be there is the result of thinking about you as an intentional system. Like Molière's M. Jourdain, know it or not, we have been speaking intentional systems all our lives. And we can say to Daniel Dennett, as M. Jourdain does to *his* philosophy tutor, "I am more obliged than anyone in the world to you for having taught me that."[57]

Lasting Lies

There are classes of idealizations that do present themselves as rough drafts, yearning for emendation, hoping to have their "deviations corrected"—mere heuristic accommodations to the abacus currently at hand. But the value of an idealization isn't to be assessed only by the accuracy of its predictions; and not all theories are empirical in nature. As we have seen, one thing an idealization can do is not so much to save the phenomena as to *explain* the phenomena. Habermas, in his early work, talked about "knowledge-constitutive interests," and thought that those interests, in the natural sciences, were about technical control. But the natural sciences have broader interests, too. Indeed, there is a range of virtues that an idealization might exhibit. A model might provide a unified account of a variety of phenomena or it might capture the essential causes of an effect with elegant simplicity.[58] There's genuine insight in noticing a mathematical regularity in some natural phenomenon, even if the regularity becomes legible only through a loss of exactitude. Some idealizations are constitutive of our concepts. Some are even flatly definitional. (Darwin's definition of adaptation can seem to be "whatever tends to help an organism survive," and then the theory of evolution by natural selection can seem like the inescapable consequence of a definition.) Vaihinger was notably skeptical of "understanding"—he thought our prospects of true understanding were sharply limited—but he entertained the possibility that "theoretical activity is or should be an end in itself for man," and all these virtues can plausibly assist our "finding our way about more easily in the world." Once we understand the range of "purposes" in this way, we see that idealizations need not be mere *faute-de-mieux* expediencies. Dennett is right that if you're playing against an electronic chess machine, you'll do better by adopting an intentional stance than by trying to work out its innards. But what if you want to *understand* how the mechanism works? Here you might want to adopt a different highly idealized model—perhaps along the lines of a network of M-P neurons—rather than drown in the details.

Indeed, philosophers in recent years have argued for just such a broader view. They have proposed that an idealization might be a means of exemplification (in Nelson Goodman's usage), as with the advantages that a line illustration may have over a photograph; or that, given the nature of certain physical systems, idealizations may be, in principle, explanatorily essential; or that one idealization may explain a phenomenon better than another that predicts it better.[59] As Michael Strevens has argued, because the object of one kind of explanation is to say what underlying causal processes produce a pattern in the world, leaving something out of the model can be justified by showing that it is causally irrelevant. So, as he points out, the fact that gas molecules hit each other can be shown to be causally irrelevant to the approximate truth of Boyle's Law, which says that the pressure and the volume of (suitably dilute) gases are inversely proportional to one another. A detailed model that includes the interactions of molecules might get you closer to the actual numbers, but it wouldn't help you understand why Boyle's Law holds.[60]

All these proposals carry the implication that an idealization's ability to explain is a virtue in its own right. And in the next chapter, I will develop a detailed account of a particular case where I think this is the correct thought, namely, the use of decision theory in trying to understand some features of our mental life. The idealization in question serves a conceptual, not an empirical, purpose. We have reason to think that our empirical theories will always turn out to be improvable; but our knowledge of our concepts can, at least sometimes, be complete already just because, like belief in belief, they are part of who we are. All along, though, we shall be proceeding in Vaihinger's shadow, following along his three main ideas: idealization involves acting in some respects as if what we know is false is true, this is justifiable because it is useful for some purpose, and the purposes in question are various.

2

A Measure of Belief

Lessons from Frank Ramsey

> The essence of pragmatism I take to be this, that
> the meaning of a sentence is to be defined by
> reference to the actions to which asserting it would
> lead, or, more vaguely still, by its possible causes
> and effects.
>
> FRANK RAMSEY,
> *Philosophical Papers*

The Ramsey Strategy

One of the most notable intellectual revolutions of
the twentieth century was the vast growth in the use
of the mathematics of probability. In the quantum
revolution, our physics became irreducibly probabilistic. So one of the central discoveries of our time
is that an event can have an objective probability,
and not just in the sense that it belongs to a class of

events that occur with a certain long-run fre-
quency: there can be single-case probabilities of an
ontologically robust kind.[1] But equally important
has been the explosion of applications of the idea of
subjective probability, the use of the mathematics
of probability to characterize a measure of the
strength of our beliefs.

The idea of subjective probability is, in the first
instance, the idea that belief comes by measurable
degrees. Philosophers have taken up this idea in
confirmation theory, seeing that subject as the study
of how evidence should lead us to align our degrees
of belief if we are to be epistemically rational; and
we have also adopted the apparatus of decision
theory, which now also plays a leading role in the
social sciences and psychology, to think about
human agency. It is a deep and interesting puzzle
why the same family of mathematical structures
can be used to regiment the objective probabilities
of physics, the subjective probabilities of decision
theory, and the idea of relative frequencies in the
long run: and one strand in the philosophy of probability has rightly focused on that question.[2]

But there is a different question in the philosophy
of probability that I started thinking about more
than thirty years ago; indeed, I sketched an answer

to it in my doctoral dissertation. It is the epistemological question how we can ground ascriptions of degrees of belief to people in publicly available evidence about their behavior and their states of mind. It is a question Richard Braithwaite, whom I mentioned in Chapter 1 in connection with the philosophy of religion, worked on in his later years: the question how subjective probabilities can be taken up in a broadly empiricist framework.

Even if belief comes by degrees, and even if those degrees of belief are somehow reflected in our heads, we clearly know no way of accessing them by looking at the brain. Furthermore, though we are often clear about what we believe, we don't often have introspective access to the degrees of our beliefs. Subjective probabilities, it seems, are themselves known, if at all, only with probability. I can in special cases announce, say, that I believe to degree 0.5 that the coin will turn up heads. But I can't decide with confidence, for example, whether I believe (unlike all those "birthers") to degree 0.98 that America's forty-fourth president was born in Hawaii. And even if I could, how could anyone *else* confirm that what I said was so?

There is now a standard answer to that question, which owes its shape to the work of Braithwaite's friend and colleague Frank Ramsey.[3] The standard answer actually owes two debts to Ramsey. The first is a broader debt. Ramsey identified a general strategy for explaining the relationship between people's behavior and their inner lives, in a way that was a great advance on the behaviorist idea that mental states were dispositions to act in response to stimuli. The strategy was developed to help think about occult phenomena generally—objects and events, like other people's beliefs and desires, that we could not directly experience or observe, but whose existence we nevertheless seemed irrevocably committed to. That challenge was central to the philosophy of science after the First World War, in the period when Ramsey (who died in 1930 at the age of twenty-six) did his work. It was instantiated in the famous problem of theoretical entities: How, they were asking in Vienna, can we combine empiricism—the thesis that claims about the world must be grounded in evidence, based on observation—with belief in unobservable entities, such as electrons or genes or the velocity of money, entities that are proposed by the very sciences whose success seems to be one of the arguments for empiricism?

Ramsey's answer was to say that these entities could be identified in a language that used only observational terms and logical apparatus. And he gave, as I said, a general strategy for doing just that, a strategy that took advantage of the fact that our understanding of the unobservable world is encompassed in a holistic scheme—the network of thoughts that Quine was to say (taking up a metaphor from a great anthropologist) were expressed in the whole web of our beliefs. This strategy still bears his name: it is the strategy of constructing what we call the "Ramsey sentence" of a theory.[4]

In the case of the mind, as we saw in Chapter 1, the relevant theory was what we now call "folk psychology." The procedure there can be described simply enough (though actually implementing it would be impossibly complex). We first assemble all the claims we are committed to about mental states and their connections with things that happen around the agent and things that the agent does. (This is the first practical impossibility.) We then join them all together with "ands" to make one very long sentence, expressing what we could call our theory of the mind. (This is a second.) Call that sentence "M" . . . for "mind." From M, we then take out all the mental terms and replace each one with the same distinct variable. (If we replace "sensation of red" with "x" in one place, we must replace every reference to that sensation with the same variable,

"x.") The result of this would be what logicians call an open sentence, which I will therefore dub "open-M." Finally, for each variable, "x," we should write "There exists an x . . ." in front of open-M, and we would have a new sentence, which didn't have any mental terms in it. That sentence is the Ramsey sentence of the theory M.

The Ramsey sentence of M says, in effect, that something that has a mind has a large number of internal states—one for each variable—that interact with input and with each other in certain specific ways, to produce behavior. It permits us to define away our mental terms in an observational language.[5] Applying Ramsey's strategy to our folk theories of the mind, you get one version of what is now called *functionalism*: the thesis that we can say what mental states *are* by characterizing their causal role as intermediaries between experience and behavior.[6]

That was the first of Ramsey's contributions. It was to suggest that if we could find a sufficiently rich body of propositions about these occult degrees of belief and the other objects or events, in and outside the mind, with which they interacted, we could define them collectively by constructing the Ramsey sentence of that theory. Behaviorism wanted to define mental states in observational terms one at a time: as functions from stimuli to responses. This was a bad idea, because what response a particular belief or desire will generate depends on your other beliefs and desires. But Ramsey showed how you could in principle do it if you proceeded holistically, defining them, in effect, together or all at once.

His second contribution was specific to degrees of belief. Ramsey showed how you could elicit evidence about people's degrees of belief from a rather specific domain of their behavior: namely, their propensity to accept and reject bets at various odds. And modern subjective probability theory begins when Ramsey develops (in a way that, I believe, was discovered at roughly the same time by the Italian mathematician Bruno de Finetti) a perfectly general method of doing this and shows that if you use that method, degrees of belief will, indeed, conform to the shape of probability functions.[7]

Later on, theorists developed a much *more* general way of doing this, which didn't require you to offer people bets. It was to show that *if* people could rank states of the world or propositions according to their preferences, so that, for every pair of states of the world, A and B, they either preferred A to B, or B to A, or were indifferent between them; and *if* that preference ranking had certain very natural seeming properties, like transitivity, then there was at least one probability function defined over those propositions that allowed you to generate their preferences as the product of degrees of belief and utilities (or something very like them). Results like these are called representation theorems.[8]

Notice what a representation theorem does and does not show. It doesn't show that we can ground degrees of belief in actual behavior. That's because, to do that, we'd have to be able to elicit the preference ranking—it would have to show up in *actual* behavior, in what economists call "revealed preferences." And there are plenty of features of your preference ranking—relating, for example, to past events, or events in the remote future—where it's not obvious that anyone is in a position to do that. Furthermore, eliciting one feature of your preferences will very often rule out revealing others. I can't *at the same time* require you to choose pairwise between apples and oranges and between bananas and pears, so finding out how you currently rank one over the other in the first pair rules out eliciting your current ranking of the other pair. Holistic ascription of this sort is bound to be like that, as is evident once you think about the general Ramsey-sentence strategy.

But though the representation theorem method doesn't mean we can ground ascriptions of degrees of belief in actual behavior, it does solve the problem that Ramsey aimed to solve. It shows that degrees of belief are an empirically respectable idea, because it allows us to say what it is for a person to have a certain degree of belief in terms of the observationally respectable idea of their preferences. We do know, for any pair of options, what it would be for someone to show that they preferred A to B: when faced with the choice between A and B, they would, on reflection, opt for A. ("The primitive sign of wanting," Elizabeth Anscombe wrote in *Intention*, "is trying to get.")[9]

Just so, the fact that we can explain occult fragility in terms of the observable idea of *breaking* makes fragility an idea that empiricists can live with, even when fragility itself is not "directly observable." The point is that a plausible empiricism requires only a disciplined connection between observation and occult properties, and not the verificationist idea, associated with some of the logical positivists, that we must be able actually to confirm every ascription of an occult property.[10] Because the idea that beliefs have a measurable strength is not part of common sense, by the way, Ramsey's proposal is best understood, I think, as showing us how to *add* the idea of subjective probability to our repertory of psychological concepts in a manner an empiricist could endorse, not as the elucidation of a previously existing folk concept.

So, though I think there are many hard and interesting problems to reflect on here, I am basically content with this Ramseyan strategy for connecting degrees of belief with behavior.

The Problem in Practice

The trouble is not with the strategy. The trouble is whether we can execute it, not for imaginary rational agents, but for actual ones. And this brings me, once more, back to the problems I wanted to focus on in this book. For here's the thing: There is overwhelming evidence that everybody we know fails to have the kind of preference ordering that is required for the representation theorems to work. And that's because there is overwhelming evidence, as I said in Chapter 1, that we aren't fully rational in the way the strategy requires.

I have been using the word "rational" so far, as Dennett did, as if it were obvious what this means. Rationality, I have assumed, involves having the beliefs you ought to have and doing what you ought to do given the beliefs and desires that you have. But it's worth insisting that "rationality" here is a term of art. The idea of rationality that is assumed in much philosophical writing on these topics is modeled on the sort of calculating abilities required for success in mathematics and logic. (The prototype here might be Mr. Spock in *Star Trek* or, even better, Data, his android successor.) This is different from the notion of reasonableness that we are using when we ordinarily judge people reasonable or unreasonable. People can and do meet this ordinary standard of reasonableness, which involves, for example, an openness to evidence, a willingness to consider other points of view, a capacity for seeing and adopting available means to their ends, and, as well, having ends that are themselves not too peculiar. A reasonable person, in this sense, is someone whose cognitive orientation is one that will make her likely, in the normal circumstances of human life, to do a pretty good job of managing her relations with other people and with the nonhuman world. No actual person, on the other hand, will meet the technical notion of rationality. So let me make it explicit that from now on I will be making arguments in this chapter using this technical notion of the rational, reserving the word "reasonable" and its cognates for the more familiar everyday notion.[11]

And let's remind ourselves how different rationality is from reasonableness. To begin with, on the side of *practical* rationality, our expressed preferences are often intransitive, so that, for example, people who would pass the test for reasonableness sometimes prefer candidate A to candidate B, and candidate B to candidate C, but don't prefer candidate A to candidate C, as Amos Tversky found when he asked a group of Harvard students to make pairwise choices between candidates for admission to college.[12] And then, on the side of *theoretical* rationality, we often believe strongly that one thing is true while strongly believing things that entail that it isn't. My favorite recent example of this is in a paper that showed that conspiracy-minded people who believed that Princess "Diana faked her own death so that she and Dodi could retreat into isolation" were likely to agree that "One or more rogue 'cells' in the British secret service constructed and carried out a plot to kill Diana." Their taste for conspiracy led them to endorse conspiracies that left Diana, like Schrödinger's cat, in a sort of superposition of dead and alive.[13] I grant that there is something slightly puzzling (if too familiar) about this frame of mind, but these views were held by people who might well have met our ordinary standards of reasonableness.

Some people suppose that this is a small problem, one that we can usually ignore. But if—as the functionalist strategy requires—to have degrees of belief just *is* to have states that work holistically together in this way to produce preferences and so action, then, if we don't have states that work holistically together in this way, we don't have degrees of belief; and all the uses to which they are put in confirmation theory or in rational choice models are, at the very best, a useful fiction; a fiction whose usefulness, if we could establish it, would be rather puzzling. After the grand debacle of the Great Recession, where so many macroeconomists got it wrong, I suppose it would be nice to be able to have a general and abstract argument against most of modern economic theory. But I want to explore some ideas that might let them off this hook, at least. And we can't do that by saying that our fundamental irrationality is a small problem.

Deep Waters

To see why the problem is deep and not shallow, let me sketch one way that we might begin to construct an account of the functional role of degrees of belief. We will clearly need more than just their role in decision and action—in producing behavioral *output*. That's because another of the functional roles of degrees of belief is to be shaped by sensation and perception, to be the result of characteristic forms of *input*: they show up as causes, for sure, but also, as a functionalist would expect, as effects.

So another ingredient we need is a precise account of how evidence leads to changes in belief. One favorite possibility here is some sort of generalized conditionalization, of the kind Richard Jeffrey suggested a while ago.[14] The details don't matter for my purposes. Let's just say for now that to conditionalize is to change from an initial probability function to a new one while keeping certain conditional probabilities constant. Jeffrey's way of doing this, let me stress, is just one of many ways of doing it. So add whatever you think is necessary to characterize the ways in which evidence impinges rationally on degrees of belief.

But whatever the details, most people who use subjective probabilities nowadays (in the sorts of ways that decision theorists do) have the idea, as I say, that we can ground our ascriptions of them in behavior;

and that this can be done in some sort of function-alist way. So how is it actually supposed to go?

The strategy, being holistic, defines subjective probabilities and the strength of desires (which, following Jeffrey, I'm going to call "desirabilities") at the same time through their connections to the way their preferences shift in response to new evidence. Roughly, then, it goes like this:

> Someone has degrees of belief and desires $<P, D>$ iff whenever they were given new evidence, they would
>
> (a) adjust from the probability function P to a probability function P', got by conditionalizing; and
>
> (b) they would next assign new desirabilities to actions, by calculating their new expected desirabilities; and
>
> (c) they would then do the available action with the highest desirability.

Nobody, least of all me, would want to take anything like this too seriously. It is hard to put the whole of decision theory and subjective probability kinematics into a single complex multiply quantified conditional. But the idea is straightforward, and it is the familiar functionalist idea: Write the Ramsey sentence of the combined decision theory and probability kinematics. I'll call that combined theory the *Economists' Model*, for short.

Suppose we did that. What should we have? Well—and this fact is extremely well known—if your favorite decision theory is anything like the theory that is implicit in most neoclassical economics (hence the name), it will have the following consequence:

> Degrees of belief and desire for all logically equivalent propositions are the same.

That requires an impossibly difficult form of coherence: you must never make a single logical mistake. It follows that we can only use the theory to ascribe degrees of belief to a creature that is fantastically rational in ways we have already agreed that you and I are not and could not be.

Introducing Idealization

There is a large literature on ways of responding to this difficulty. But my interest in these pages is in trying to understand and explore one particular, popular, and I think quite helpful response. It is the response that says that the application of these ideas to actual people involves an idealization:

> Idealization for the Economists' Model: An agent's degrees of belief and desire are characterized by the behavior to which they would lead in a— conceptually related—fictional agent of a certain idealized kind, and not by the behavior of that actual agent.

And the first challenge in making sense of this response is relatively straightforward, because it is the standard problem with idealization. If the agent doesn't behave in the way the model requires, what does it mean to say that we can understand her by proceeding *as if* she did? Treating the model as an idealization means that we don't have to worry that it gets things wrong. For, again, *an idealization is just a kind of useful fiction.* And a fiction is something that isn't true, but that we treat for certain purposes as if it were. In Chapter 1, I asked why we should be happy with a theory once we knew that it wasn't true. Shouldn't we be in the business of looking further for one that is? How can it be useful to have a theory whose predictions we know will often be false?

A Little Deck Clearing

Let me return to, and put aside, a couple of answers here. One is that in saying that the theory is idealized we are saying it is approximately true; and that, in this, it is like all other theories about measurable quantities. But this isn't an idea we can very easily extend from, say, the gas laws to the case of the mind. For we don't have a measure of distance from the theory's predictions. What the theory predicts are actions—and you either do them or you don't. If the pattern of actions doesn't fit with the theory, you can't assign a measure to the degrees of belief at all.

So you might try a different strategy. You might suppose, instead, that a theory that makes all-or-nothing predictions is approximately right if it is right more often than not, or mostly or almost all the time. But none of these conditions obtains for our decision theory, for a simple reason: consistency, at least as it is conceived of in standard decision theories, is an all-or-nothing matter. Once you admit to the system a couple of beliefs or desires that are logically equivalent but distinct in probability or desirability, the theory allows you to predict every action—and thus none.

Ah, you say, but there is another way in which we might give sense to the notion of the theory's being approximately true. The theory might assign degrees of belief that are close to the *actual* degrees of belief; then it would be approximately true, to the extent that the values it assigned were near to the actual values. This won't help with the problem at hand, however. I am supposing that the only way we know of to give sense to a numerical measure of degrees of belief is by way of the Economists' Model. If the theory is false of actual agents, it can't be approximately true in this way. For to carry through this thought we'd need something we don't have: namely, a way of measuring degrees of belief independently of seeing actions show up in response to evidence and seeing what degrees of belief would produce those responses, if decision theory were true.

In other words, you can't say that a theory that allows you to measure something (in this case, belief) is approximately right, unless you have some other way of measuring, which gives you values to compare with. We don't have that other way of measuring. The only candidates here seem to be essentially phenomenological notions of the strength of belief (the distinctness of Cartesian ideas, the forcefulness of Humean impressions), notions that correlate very poorly with the notion of strength of conviction that is implicit in decision theory. My firm belief that there are apple trees in the orchard doesn't have a "feel" that is much different from my weaker conviction that I remembered to feed the ducks. And certainly nothing in my conscious consideration of these two questions—"Apple trees in the orchard?" and "Appiah fed the ducks?"—reveals to me a mathematical value for the strength of my beliefs. So idealization of the sort we are dealing here is a different problem from approximation.

Here's another response to the question of what is going on in a descriptive theory that usually fails to predict what an agent will do. It's to say that the theory has a *ceteris paribus* clause specifying that it is to apply only when circumstances are in certain ways standard. Thus, the temporary presence of phytocannabinoids in my brain may reasonably permit us to excuse the theory's failure to explain what I do, because the environment (in this case the "milieu intérieur") in which I am operating, is one in which the *cetera* are not *paria*. The idea here is that the theory is true *within a certain limited range of environments*. But many of the failures of rationality that occur in normal human beings are—as

Christopher Cherniak argued so persuasively a couple of decades ago—the consequence of features of our normal situation, such as our computational finitude and our limited memory. Our rational failures are mostly not accounted for by temporary aberrations.[15] Ordinary reasonableness has to be consistent with forgetfulness and the very substantial limits of our capacity for logical inference.

And so, to return to the main line of the argument, I ask again: What is it *in this case* that allows us to find useful a theory whose predictions we know will often be false?

Truth under Idealized Assumptions

Well, to say that a theory idealizes is to treat it, Vaihinger taught us, as conditional upon certain counterfactual assumptions: If certain false propositions were true, then the consequences of the theory would follow. Newton's first law tells us what would happen to any body in a forceless universe. But, of course, there isn't any such body. Counterfactuals about the physically impossible forceless universe are what nevertheless make the law true.

The way to proceed with degrees of belief and desire is to suppose that they are properties of beliefs and desires that are characterized by the way an agent would behave if, counterfactually, he or she were what I call computationally perfect, in a sense I shall now try to explain. Computational perfection characterizes more precisely the counterfactual assumptions we need to get going with subjective probability theories.

But to do this I shall need first to say what I mean when I say that a theory of mental states is computational. A computational theory treats beliefs as representations; and it says that some mental processes are computations with these and other representations. Beliefs and desires, then, are representations that have properties reflecting, respectively, the degree of the belief and the strength of the desire. What makes the account computational is that, along with probabilities and desirabilities, these representations also have *computational structures:* properties whose functional significance is that the outcome of certain mental processes—the computations—is the production of a new state whose computational structure is a function of the computational structures of the preexisting "input" states. So, to put the point in a more familiar way, beliefs and desires have something analogous to syntax for sentences: they have form as well as content.

What is required by a computational theory of decision is that our minds are so constituted that, given these materials—probabilities, desirabilities, and computational structures—they compute the expected desirabilities that underlie our actions: producing, that is, those states immediately anterior to action in such a way that their computational structures and desirabilities are determined by the probabilities, desirabilities, and computational structures of antecedent beliefs and desires.[16]

Computation, so conceived, is a mental process, a process that is carried out in us by our central nervous systems, and that, like all processes, takes time. And it is a process that can also go wrong, a process in which computational errors can occur. If the computations are completed, though, the agent comes to be in a state of preferring some options to others and this (modulo problems in her motor system) will cause her to do the most preferred basic actions; and if the computation is without error as well as complete, then that action will be a basic action with maximum desirability. There are thus, on this view, two obvious barriers to an agent's action displaying her preferences as computed by the Economists' Model. First, the necessary computations might not be carried out; second, there might be some error in the computation.

Normal Functioning

This does not mean that we can now treat anything at all as an agent, by regarding all deviations from predicted behavior as computational errors. Why isn't this table, you might ask, possessed of computational states that it just doesn't happen to carry out? The answer: Computational errors must be *deviations from the normal functioning of the physical system* that embodies the functional states. It follows that in calling something a computational error we are committed to there being some explanation of it. A deviation from normal functioning is, indeed, a deviation from what is prescribed by the theory. But this is not circular. What it means is that if the agent's behavior deviates from what the theory requires, this must be the result of an *independently specifiable causal intervention* with her mental functioning. As Nancy Cartwright once said (apropos of idealization in physics):

> In calling something an idealization it seems not so important that the contributions from omitted

factors be small, but that they be ones for which we know how to correct. If the idealization is to be of use, when the time comes to apply it to a real system we had better know how to add back the contributions of the factors that have been left out . . . either the omitted factors do not matter much or we know how to treat them.[17]

Cartwright's thought is that good physics can generally be quite bad at predicting lots of things because each physical theory captures some—but only some—of the properties of objects; and to make the best predictions about an object, you'd have to capture all of the relevant properties at once. Mostly we can't do that. If the only property of objects were their mass, a good theory of gravitation and dynamics would allow us to predict their motions. But there are many forces acting on every object apart from gravitational ones. To predict the movement of a feather, we need to know about friction, wind, static electrical forces, and no doubt a whole lot else. (And that's assuming it is not attached to a bird.) To predict the movement of a person, we'll usually need to know about some psychological capacities as well—though not if she is a parachutist in free fall. So we're not worried when the predictions are wrong if we have some idea about why.

Consider the parallel with a simpler case, that of the "theory" of the thermostat. We can continue to treat a system as a thermostat when it is not *functioning* as one, provided there is some causal process interfering—a process that is both specifiable otherwise than as "whatever is causing the interference" and one in whose absence the system would work as the functional laws governing thermostats require. (There might, for example, be an electrical storm interfering with a heat-sensor.) Analogous possibilities exist for agents. For example, in paralysis. Here there is a causal fact about the agent's musculature, which interferes with the route from belief and desire to action, and in whose absence the agent would do what the functionalist theory requires.[18]

This, then, is a sketch of how we might implement the idea that the *ceteris paribus* clauses, which specify the decision-theoretic features of belief and desire, require the circumstances to be normal.

Cognitive Angels, Again

The relevant idealization requires, then, that the Economists' Model should take no account of computations, but should assume that all the computations necessary to calculate expected desirability have been carried out. Though the formal theory is called a decision theory, you could say that the Economists' Model takes no account of the process of decision: takes no account of the actual causal processes by which an agent comes to give highest priority to doing one particular thing. The reason the Economists' Model is unable to distinguish beliefs with the same truth conditions is thus simply stated: If an agent has a belief that S, and this is logically equivalent to a belief that R, then the Economists' Model assumes, in effect, that the agent has carried out the computations necessary to discover this, and assigned R the probability that S has. I am claiming, then, that the Economists' Model characterizes the behavior of those computationally perfect agents I earlier called Cognitive Angels.

So let me state the point starkly: The Economists' Model characterizes the behavior of an agent (with the appropriate concepts) who applies each one of the computations that she is physically capable of applying, instantaneously and without error. Call this class of computations that a Cognitive Angel with the appropriate concepts can perform, the set of *feasible computations with those concepts*. The idealization involved requires that there be, for any agent, the Cognitive Angel to which he or she is related—the one with the same concepts. The feasible computations for an individual are the feasible computations with her concepts; those being the feasible computations with those concepts determined by the related Cognitive Angel.[19]

So: It is part of this conception of the functional role of degrees of belief and desire that, if an agent were computationally perfect, he or she would act in the way the Economists' Model requires. For example, the Economists' Model tells us what it is, in part, to believe to such and such a degree that snow is white, by saying what agents with a belief of that degree would do, given all their other beliefs and desires, if they carried out all the computations necessary to calculate expected desirability. No actual agents are computationally perfect, but the states that determine their actual behavior can still be characterized by how they would manifest themselves, given computational perfection. Analogously, the actual velocities of real gas molecules, which explain their less-than-ideal actual behavior, may nevertheless be characterized as the velocities that would, if only gas molecules were perfectly inelastic point masses, produce the ideal gas laws predicted by the simplest version of the kinetic theory of gases.

The Problem of Contradictory Fictions Reconsidered

In assuming computational perfection in characterizing probability and desirability, we are supposing that, given sufficient computational effort, a preference ranking of the right kind would result. Given the sort of representation theorems I mentioned earlier, there will be reason to think agents *will* adjust their states in ways that tend to produce acceptable preference orderings, so long as we can show that where agents realize that their degrees of belief do not conform to the probability axioms, and their desirabilities fail to conform to the desirability logic, they must in fact so adjust them as to remove this defect.

But isn't it simply a condition of our making sense of agents that we think they would remove inconsistencies of this kind if they came to their notice? If a creature were to come to believe strongly that S, and to believe strongly that not S, and was aware that this was its situation, we could only continue to treat it as possessing those beliefs if it made some adjustment to remove the plain inconsistency, precisely because it became aware of it. So far, so good.

Now, here's a problem, one that Vaihinger would have anticipated. In the case of beliefs and desires, this strategy won't really work, for a simple reason: The antecedents of the counterfactuals, which define the Cognitive Angel, are not contingently impossible, they are logically impossible. It is not merely contingently true that I don't compute all consequences of my beliefs instantaneously and without error. If it were, computation wouldn't be what it is: a process. This means that evaluating the truths about Cognitive Angels involves assessing counterfactuals with impossible antecedents: and in the current state of play in logical theory, that takes you into territory that is very hard to make sense of. We are back, in other words, with the difficulty I discussed regarding Vaihinger's idea of the fiction as conditional upon an impossibility.

Weakening the Constraints

What can we do about this? I suggest that there are a few thoughts that we might start off from. First, we might simply try a less extreme kind of idealization.

Thus, we might propose that the relevant conditionals are not of the form:

> If the agent's computations took no time and the agent made no errors, . . .

but instead are of the form:

> If the agent's computations were speeded up, and there were no errors, . . .

And this looks hopeful. Normally our explanation of why an actual agent deviates from the behavior of a Cognitive Angel relies on supposing that there is some set of computations (often a small set) that would, if they had been carried out correctly and without error, have led that agent to do what a Cognitive Angel would have done.[20]

Notice that the approach I am proposing here is essentially an application of Nancy Cartwright's thought, which I cited earlier: "If the idealization is to be of use, when the time comes to apply it to a real system we had better know how to add back the contributions of the factors that have been left out." On my proposal, what's "left out" of the decision-theoretic treatment is the fact that mental states are representations, with form as well as content, syntax as well as semantics: they represent a way the world might be, but they represent it in one of many possible ways. And when people don't do what is decision-theoretically rational—and the explanation isn't that there's a temporary instability in the brain—appeal to the fact that they have limited memories and capacities for computation can turn out to be just the factor we have left out.

But a Cognitive Angel would never have developed a set of beliefs that was inconsistent or preferences that were intransitive. And speeding up the processes here will only get you more quickly to the point where the agent is reaching contradictions, and then the theory will be of no use in telling us what the agent would do, because it will predict that it does anything and everything. Stepping back from full perfection will work only with sets of beliefs and desires that are fully rational. We are committed, therefore, to an account that says what each state is by understanding what its behavior would be in a system of states embodied in a fully rational person. So the idealization in question cannot be one that relates an actual agent to a single Cognitive Angel: rather, each of her actual states is understood by way of the role it would play in a different Cognitive Angel, whose states are coherent. This is because the only way to make sense of the incoherence of our mental states is as the product of the interaction of coherent families, in the way that I suggested earlier we should borrow from David Lewis.

Williamson's Objection

There is a related challenge to the counterfactual approach I have adopted here, one raised by Timothy Williamson in his book *Knowledge and Its Limits*, drawing on earlier work by R. K. Shope.[21] Williamson says (of a slightly different proposal):

> It fails in the way in which counterfactual analyses usually fail, by ignoring side-effects of the conditional's antecedent on the truth-value of the analysandum.

What he has in mind is that, very often, a fully rational being wouldn't have the beliefs (or desires or preferences) that an actual person has. As a result, we cannot give an account of what it is to be in certain states of mind in terms of what a fully rational person would be like, because a fully rational person couldn't be in that state of mind. Williamson's basic example here is a simple one. You cannot say what it would be for a person to believe "I am not fully rational" by discussing what a fully rational person would do if they had it: a fully rational person wouldn't have it. And you'd be back considering a counterfactual's truth-value in an impossible circumstance.

But we don't need to give up so quickly. It's true that we can't give an account in these terms of what it is to believe something that a fully rational agent would not believe. But it should have been obvious all along that we couldn't give such a counterfactual analysis this way for beliefs that are *a priori* false. For a belief that's *a priori* false is one that a fully rational agent would know to be false. So we can't give an account of what it is to believe (to such-and-such a degree) something that is *a priori* false by saying what it would lead a perfectly rational agent to do.

We need, then, to take out from actual agents' representations any *a priori* falsehoods and any other beliefs that a rational agent wouldn't have because she would know that she was a rational agent. I'll call these the *irrationals*; the rest are the *rationals*. We are aiming to exclude cases where, as Williamson put it, we know that the conditional's antecedent will have side effects on the truth-value of the analysandum.

Limiting yourself to the rationals means that if you wanted to give degrees of belief to irrationals, you would have to understand them in some other way.[22] That is not so surprising, though, once you think about it. Generally speaking, once we recognize that a belief is *a priori* false, we have a hard time figuring out what someone who had that belief should do. We can still say what it would be to have such and such a degree of belief for all the other rational propositions by saying what a computationally perfect agent would do who had a probability and desirability function defined over the rationals. Vaihinger taught us, after all, that the heart of idealization is leaving some things out.[23]

Idealization and Normativity

Sometimes people respond to the empirical difficulties of the Economists' Model by conceding that it is, indeed, false, but that this is because it constitutes a normative ideal. What the Economists' Model is for, on this view, is not predicting or describing behavior—not even the behavior of an idealized agent—but saying how we *should* ideally behave.

If this is meant as an account of the sense in which the decision theories that modern functionalists have wanted to use idealize human behavior, then it is just a *pun* to say that they do so by providing ideals we should live up to. I am discussing the role of the Economists' Model as part of a descriptive account of human beliefs and desires, and in this context it will do no good to defend the theory from its empirical inadequacies by observing that it would be a better world if people did conform to the theory. To make this move is just to give up claiming a role for the Economists' Model in structuring *descriptive* psychological theories.

Still, the question of the relation between normative accounts of psychological states and descriptive psychological theories—the relation in this domain between idealization and ideals—deserves some attention. Christopher Peacocke, in his book *Thoughts*, said at one point: "The identity of a content is determined by certain normative conditions relating to acceptance of the content."[24] And he then averred that this normativity entails that the account of content he proposed does not belong to cognitive psychology, because cognitive psychology is a non-normative empirical pursuit. But Peacocke also insisted that it does *not* follow that the entities individuated by the normative theory of content cannot be the very same entities discussed in cognitive psychology; for, as he says, "there may be supervenience of the contents, normatively individuated, of a subject's states upon the characterizations given by an empirical psychology of that subject which employs descriptions relating him to his environment."[25]

I think this is true enough. But what is missing so far is any sense that the connection between normative and descriptive theories is more than accidental. If we understood this connection a little better, we might be able better to understand the role of the descriptive idealizations of psychological theories.

Conforming to the Norms

To begin with, there is one obvious way that the normative and descriptive theories are related. The descriptive theory allows us to define the degrees of belief and desirabilities about which the normative theory makes recommendations. If we *should* conform to the classical decision theory, we *should* assign our degrees of belief, for example, in such a way that their measure has the shape of a probability function. But to do that, we need to know what degrees of belief are—and that is exactly what the Ramsey-style theory, construed as I have construed it, does. *Whether* we should try to conform to the norms of the pure classical theory is another question. But here, too, the idealizing functionalist theory helps. For it allows us to explore what might happen if we did try; and I shall suggest in a moment that, once we explore this question, we can see that classical decision theory is not a set of ideals worth our trying to conform to.

There are always descriptive facts about what norms individuals and societies respect. If Peacocke is right, it is a fact about us, *qua* possessors of certain concepts, that we think that people should accept certain judgments on the basis of such-and-such evidence; and that we also believe that, once we have accepted those judgments, we are rationally committed to other judgments. Nevertheless, it is clear that the contents of these beliefs—beliefs about what one should do or about what one is rationally committed to believing—are not reducible without residue to accounts of non-normative fact. You don't understand what it is for something to be rationally required simply because you know how a community of people who *believed* that it was rationally required would behave.

What else is required might, perhaps, be put as a slogan: To know what it is for something to be rationally required is to recognize the demands of reason. Less programmatically: To know what it is for something to be rationally required is to be disposed, once you see that an act, A, is, indeed, rationally required, to try to behave—other things, as usual, being equal—as is rationally required; to be disposed, then, to do A. Looked at this way, the particular mode of idealization I have proposed is bound to seem unhelpfully radical.

For to idealize in this way is to regard us as governed by the thought that we should aim to do what someone like us who was computationally perfect would find it best to do: and this is risky, because thus to ignore the fact of our manifold computational imperfections may lead us to be worse off, *by the very same standards*, than we might be if we opted for less stringent idealizations. There is no guarantee that a computationally imperfect creature that aims at the goals of a computationally perfect creature will end up doing what computational perfection would entail more often than it would if it used, say, rules of thumb that recognized its imperfections and used its knowledge of its own place in the world.

I may well do better in the long run, for example, by refusing complex bets from a smart Dutch

bookmaker at large odds than by trying to calculate in every case what pattern of acceptance will
maximize my expected gains. And in recent years a
whole field has grown up in the formal and empirical study of heuristics, strategies of thought whose
adoption by creatures in a world like ours and with
limited memories and computational (and other
cognitive) capacities like ours will lead them very
often to do what their computationally ideal
counterparts would judge best.

What this thought suggests is that the mode of
idealization appropriate to developing strategies for
real-life decision making should be different from
the mode I have adopted here; and this naturally
invites the question "For what purposes is *this* mode
of idealization appropriate?"

One place where it is appropriate is in trying to
understand the different roles of the contents (the
truth conditions) and the forms (the computational
structures) of our beliefs in characterizing their
functional roles. That classical decision theory
helps for these purposes does not guarantee that it
is apt for others: indeed, once we understand how
radical this mode of idealization is, it will be clear
that we should *not* adopt it for practical decision

making. Our knowledge of ourselves allows us to recognize both the conceptual possibility of a kind of rationality—that of the Cognitive Angel—and at the same time the fact that it is not possible for us. Paradoxically, then, the recognition that our decision-theoretic picture is an idealization comes with the recognition that it is of no use, for us, as an ideal at which to aim.[26]

Back to the Economists' Model

In sum, the mode of idealization in the Economists' Model—the picture of human agency embedded in treating people as utility-maximizing rational agents—essentially ignores the actual computational processes that produce new representations: beliefs, desires, intentions, and the like. Computation depends on the form of representations, treating the belief that it's not raining or not snowing as distinct from the belief that it's not both raining and snowing—as different, that is, for processing purposes—even though their contents (the states of the world that would make them true) are demonstrably identical. Form and content exhaust the properties representations *must* have *as* representations, though, like sentences on paper or coming out of your mouth, they will have myriad other properties as well.

Let's call the causal powers of representations that relate to their form their *logical* powers and the ones that relate to their content their *conceptual* powers. By the content of a representational state I mean, roughly, what Frege called, for beliefs, the *thoughts* (Gedanken) they express. So, to stick with his famous example, the contents of the *belief that the Morning Star is Venus* and the *belief that the Evening Star is Venus* will be different, even if, because the Morning Star *is* the Evening Star, these two beliefs will be true in exactly the same possible worlds. Philosophical semantics has engaged a good deal over the last few decades with the question how to relate these two conceptions of content: the Fregean one and the possible-worlds one. This book is not the place to examine that question. So I need to make it clear that the notion of content that I'm relying on here is (closer to) the Fregean one. Naturally we will need a notion of a way the world might have been as well; but because, on the Fregean view, there are thoughts that represent the world in ways it could not have been, the Fregean notion of content is not one captured by specifying in what possible worlds a representation is true.[27]

One of what we call "Frege's Puzzles," then, is a challenge to what might seem an obvious thought about the contents of thoughts, namely:

> CONTENT: that beliefs have the same content if and only if, when either is true, the other must be true, too.

As I've just reminded you, this claim is false because "The Morning Star is the Evening Star" must be true just in case "The Evening Star is the Evening Star" is true, yet these two have different contents. My response to this challenge isn't to say how I think Frege's Puzzle can be solved. Rather, it's to insist (a) that we need such a notion of content, (b) that there must be some solution to Frege's Puzzle, but (c) that CONTENT, precisely for this reason, cannot be true. What *is* true of my notion of content is this:

> CONTENT*: that beliefs have the same content if and only if, when either is true, it is possible to infer validly that the other is true, too.

This claim does not fall victim to Frege's Puzzle about the Morning and Evening Stars. It does,

however, still face the problem, which Frege identified, of treating much mathematics as being
"about" structure rather than content. I have no
contribution to make to this discussion. What we
are to say concerning beliefs about mathematical
truths that are undecidable by computation is another matter. But nobody should require us to
solve deep questions in the philosophy of mathematics before going on with our philosophical
psychology.

The causal powers of representations *as such* can
therefore be conceived of as the sum of their logical
powers and their conceptual powers; and so a theory
that leaves out—that is, idealizes away—their logical
powers displays, we could say, their conceptual
powers. It gives us a grasp on how the contents of
mental representations matter for their role in
responding to experience and determining behavior,
even when, because those powers are always embodied in states with logical powers as well, we will
never see the conceptual powers operating on their
own. Any particular embodiment of a certain
system of representations—your brain in your body
or mine in mine—will have causal properties that
are neither logical nor conceptual in this sense: the
causal properties of my current representations will

include multitudinous facts supervenient upon my particular neurophysiology. But every system of representations must have at least the logical and conceptual powers that this theory helps us to understand. Understanding the conceptual powers doesn't help very much with predicting or controlling agents; that is not the payoff of these models of rational agency, and that is why it is right to be skeptical about the likelihood that rational choice accounts will be empirically useful in a detailed way.

For example, the fact that growing demand will increase prices in a market of rational actors with a fixed supply of some good, is something we can *understand* in terms of the rational choice model, considering only the conceptual properties of human belief and desire, even though in any actual market there will be so many ways that the logical properties matter. The logical properties help explain why we often do not do what we would do if we were logically omniscient. And this understanding is worth having, even though it is quite practically unhelpful in predicting the actual track of prices through time—not least because changing patterns of demand, which we would require as input for this purpose, can be predicted only by theories that go beyond the Economists' Model.

They are exogenous variables, in the jargon. As they should be—because what makes a person come to want one thing rather than another is not determined solely by reasoning; it depends, too, on all the other processes that generate desire.

The way I have proposed for combining explanations of the conceptual and the logical properties of representations involves using a theory conditional on the false assumption that we are logically omniscient to get at the conceptual properties, and combining it with a theory that is conditional on the assumption that we are not logically omniscient to get at the logical properties. So here, too, we are bringing together in a single explanation theoretical resources that are strictly inconsistent with one another.

We have reached a point where I can underline an analogy between the treatment I am suggesting of the rational choice case and Cartwright's treatment of the idealizations of physics; for she, too, suggests that the way we build representations of physical systems to explain them involves bringing together theories that are strictly inconsistent with one another. How you do that in practice is something you learn in graduate school in physics. How you bring together our understanding of the con-

ceptual and the logical properties of beliefs and desires is something you learn as you begin to treat
other people as intentional systems. Fortunately,
this does not require training in graduate school; in
part, I think, because, as I argued at the end of
Chapter 1, most of us—though, perhaps, not some
people far out on the autism spectrum—come pro-
grammed by nature to apply a Theory of Mind.

What we see here is the intimate connection between the description of a person or community as
recognizing certain norms—a description that
might be offered from the perspective of an outsider—and the understanding of those norms from
the perspective of the member of the community,
from the point of view of the insider. And because,
in the case of descriptive decision theory, we are
attempting to characterize the norms, conformity
to which constitutes someone, for our community,
as what we call an "agent," we are addressing from
the outsider's perspective a question on which we
can always adopt, as agents in our community, the
insider's perspective. To see this is to see that an
agent is not simply a *thing* that conforms, more or
less inadequately, to the constraints of rationality
that decision theory represents, but also a *person* who
recognizes, however imperfectly, those constraints

as rationally binding. That is an attitude you can have only if you regard them as binding yourself.

In Chapter 3, I will turn to a different set of cases where a normative theory—this time, the theory of justice—relies on idealization, because it ignores general truths about the bad behavior of human beings: this time not rationally bad behavior—cognitive imperfection—but morally bad behavior—which Vaihinger, coming from that Swabian parsonage, might have seen as arising from Original Sin. But before turning to that final task, I want to say a little more about fictions in the most literal and ordinary sense of the term: the ones that you can find in the bookstore listed under mysteries, romances, or thrillers. This will give us another useful perspective on Vaihinger's story before we move on.

Make-Believe

I have been discussing one way of using subjective probability theory. It is important to stress, though, that there are many other ways of thinking about belief, some of which I discussed in Chapter 1. As I said in the Preface, one central lesson of reflection on idealization is that we humans work best with many models of the world in its immeasurable diversity. Let me point out now that our capacity for multiple representations is evident from our earliest years.

Some of the most marvelous capacities of children are so natural and so familiar that we can lose track of how extraordinary they are. One such ability, as the philosopher Kendall L. Walton taught me many years ago, is their aptitude for make-believe. Martha, in the garden, forms a shape out of the mud in her hand and tells us, if we ask, that it's a cake. If she has a toy kitchen set, she may place this "cake" in the "oven." So far, so familiar. And yet something very strange is happening here. It is another instance of the philosophy of the as-if. For she is inviting us to join her in treating something that she knows is not a cake *as if* it were. But only *in some respects.* She's not going to put it in her mouth, for she knows that this "cake" is in fact mud and that mud is no good for eating. She may blow on it when it comes out of the toy oven, because that is what you do with something that is hot. But she's not worried about being burned. Because though the cake is "hot" in her make-believe, she knows that the mud that "is" the cake is cool. Psychologists and anthropologists make a great deal, rightly, of the fact that in this sort of play children are rehearsing for real life: for real cakes that need real cooling after real cooking. But let us begin by acknowledging how strange a capacity this is, especially given that it is something children take up at a certain age with very little prompting. The child who plays at cooking does not need to be *taught* that she is not really cooking, that the mud is not a cake, that the oven is not hot, that you eat the cake by pretending to put it in your mouth. We come prebaked for make-believe.

Kendall Walton began with this fundamental capacity for as-if play, one shared by children everywhere, and drew on an understanding of it to help explore the very grown-up activity of responding to the representational arts: fiction, storytelling, drama. His insight was that there is an important connection between the play of children and these adult entertainments. When we are moved by Horatio's loyalty to Hamlet (or, for that matter, Piglet's faithfulness to Pooh), we respond, he argued, in some respects as we would if we were seeing or hearing about actual moments of personal fidelity. And yet (in the normal case), we know all the time that what we are seeing represented on the stage is not really happening or that what we are reading on the page never happened.

Borges once wrote (in a passage Walton cites) that the actor "on a stage plays at being another before a gathering of people who play at taking him for that other person."[28] His idea was that it isn't only the actor who engages in make-believe. We aren't really moved by the death of Ophelia, he wanted to say; we're pretending to be moved. The scene on the stage is a prop in our pretense, as the mud-pie is a prop in Martha's playing at cooking.[29] But if we choose, we can, at any moment, like Martha, abandon the make-believe.

I have learned that most nonphilosophers find Borges's notion—that the feelings we have when we respond to fictions are somehow fake—very hard to accept. If I weep when Ophelia dies, they want to say, it is because I am upset. I am not in any sense *pretending* to be upset. Ironically, on this natural view, though the actor may be faking her feelings, performing as if she were happy or sad or fearful or elated, the audiences' responses, if they are engaged by the drama, strike us as involving genuine feeling. There is something to this resistance to Borges's claim, I think. For one thing, the phenomenology of the emotions behind my tearful response to Ophelia's death is altogether indistinguishable from the phenomenology of my feeling at a funeral: they feel the same. Still, normally when I am sad, it is because I believe that something regrettable has really happened; but when Ophelia "dies," I am never in any doubt about whether an actual person has died. In one sense, then, it is never true that the drama involves what Coleridge called a "willing suspension of disbelief."

My sadness at Ophelia's "death" involves not an abandonment of the belief that no one has died, but abandonment of one of the normal consequences of that belief, which would be (other things being equal) that I had nothing to be sad about. That's what it is to permit myself to feel *as if* someone had died. We do not need to deny that this feels like real sadness, sadness about an actual regrettable event. But it differs from that feeling in not being associated with the kind of belief that normally makes sadness intelligible. What is suspended is not disbelief but the normal affective response to disbelief. I am reacting—but only in some respects—as if I believe an unhappy young woman has died. Someone who didn't have an appropriate response to the real event wouldn't have an appropriate response to the fictional one either.

Walton calls feelings like these quasi-emotions. (And "quasi," you will note, is the Latin for "as if.")

But they are quasi not in the sense that it is only *as if we had the emotion,* but in the sense that they are emotions that we have because it is *as if we believed something was so.*

This proposal suggests an important analogy to the case of our beliefs when we are engaging in theoretical idealization. To think about subjective probability, I just argued, we need to think of people, sometimes, as if they were logically omniscient. This involves treating them as we would if they were, in fact, logically omniscient. But again only in some respects. We sometimes treat them, that is, as if they must have seen the logical equivalence of two thoughts, though we also know that sometimes we will have to explain what they have done by recognizing that they have failed to grasp exactly that logical fact. Treating someone as a rational agent, while recognizing them to be actually irrational, is a matter of operating, if you like, with the pretense that they are rational, a pretense that is like all make-believe—bounded, so that we don't draw all its consequences. Just as my sadness at Ophelia's death involves not drawing the emotional consequence of my belief that no one in the theater has died, so when I am applying the intentional strategy I don't draw all the cognitive consequences of my belief that an agent is irrational. I suspend my disbelief in her rationality in the sense in which I suspend my disbelief that someone has died. I don't *abandon* the belief. I give up some of its normal consequences.

This capacity is possible only because our minds are *not* unified. Cognitive Angels, aware of the logical incompatibilities of their pictures, would have to resolve them by seeking a single consistent view. It is our imperfection that allows us to work, not with a single picture of the world, but with many. And because they are incompatible with one another—because they cannot all be true—we have to be able to keep them separate if we are not to be drawn into incoherence. I *can* think of the earth as spherical and as ellipsoidal, for different purposes; what I *cannot* reasonably do is think of it both ways for the same purpose and at the same time. Our knowledge of reality is held, then, in pictures of the world, each of which has something wrong with it but is good enough for some purposes. Muddling the pictures up—trying to make them into one big picture—has always been the dream of those, like Eliot's Casaubon with his *Key to All Mythologies*, who believe in the unity of all knowledge. In the twentieth century that vision was expressed in the positivist ideal of the unification of the sciences, with its goal of reducing psychology to biology, and then to chemistry and then to physics—considering physics to be the only real science because it is the most fundamental and the most general. This vision was always a vision for the long run; and it always invited the response that John Maynard Keynes made to the predictions of monetary economists about the long run: "But this *long run* is a misleading guide to current affairs. *In the long run, we're all dead.*"[30] I am not making a point about the fact that we live in the short run. I am arguing that, given the way we are, we will need to have many pictures in the long run, too; in fact, for as long as we are around. And whenever someone proposes replacing one of our many pictures with a better picture, it will always be a good idea to ask Vaihinger's question: "Better for what?" In the meantime, the great skill in managing our cognitive lives is figuring out which pictures to use for which purposes. And that, as we shall now see, is also a central challenge in political philosophy.

3

Political Ideals

Lessons from John Rawls

For the most part I examine the principles of justice
that would regulate a well-ordered society.
Everyone is presumed to act justly and to do his
part in upholding just institutions.

JOHN RAWLS,
A Theory of Justice

Four Kinds of As-Ifs in Normative Theory

In Chapter 2, I explored one way in which an idealized model—a model, in fact, of a measure of
belief—could be useful in helping us to understand
something about our actual beliefs. The idealization
in question was of a certain sort of unrealizable logical perfection; and so I offered, in effect, a model of
your and my degrees of belief based on a conception
of what belief would be like in an agent that con-

formed to that impossible ideal. The idealized model here, as Vaihinger insisted, assumes not just something false but something that *couldn't* be true. Logical perfection would require instantaneous computation: and computation, being a process, couldn't be instantaneous. We also noticed that direct attempts to live up to that ideal would likely lead to outcomes that were worse than governing our behavior by simpler, more manageable *heuristics*; heuristics that will lead us, with our actual capacities and our actual circumstances, to do very often what an ideally rational agent with our aims would do. Still, I claimed, this idealized model revealed something important about actual beliefs. It showed something about the separate roles of what I called their conceptual and logical properties.

In this chapter, I want to turn from thinking about idealizations in the philosophy of mind and action to thinking about their role in political philosophy. You can find examples of such idealizations everywhere you look. In modern political theory, for example, proposals for normative ideals of justice have been offered that defend those ideals by showing what a society would be like in which everyone conformed to them. We model our political ideals here by supposing a world in which people behave in a way that we know actual people will not.

In the pages ahead, I am going to explore four kinds of as-if thinking in moral and political theory. The first will involve a discussion of the ways in which a number of political theorists, John Rawls prominent among them, assume away certain features of human social or psychological reality in building theories of justice. Rawls introduced a notion of ideal theory to justify such practices: I want first to try to make sense of that notion.

Next, I will consider issues raised by the fact that we can build models of the world that assume away not social or scientific truths but normative ones. Thinking about counter-normative possibilities— ways the world could have been, but is not, morally—turns out to be another important kind of idealization.

Our third set of questions will be about a central feature of much modern thought about morality: namely, our persistent willingness to characterize people for moral purposes using concepts that we have officially disavowed. The paradigm here, for me, is racial thinking; but I shall argue that much discussion of sexuality shares this feature. We shall discover, too, that some of our moral talk about character can be illuminated by thinking about it, too, as a kind of idealization.

Finally, I will discuss ways in which political thought idealizes away various features of social reality in developing accounts of political morality. Here, as we shall see, there is scope for theories that ignore a variety of features of the world. Our guide here will be Vaihinger's recognition that we need to ask, not just what false claims a theory treats as true, but also for what purposes this idealization occurs. I shall argue, too, that there are reasons for skepticism about a certain familiar kind of ideal theorizing, one that seeks to guide our actions in the actual imperfect world by an image of utopia.

These, then, are the tasks ahead in thinking about idealization and ideals in moral and political theory. Let me turn to the first of them now.

An Ideal Theory of Justice

John Rawls remarked early on in A *Theory of Justice* that he was going to "examine the principles of justice that would regulate a well-ordered society." "Everyone," he continued, in adumbrating the idea of a well-ordered society, "is presumed to act justly

and to do his part in upholding just institutions."
So, he said, he was developing what he called "strict
compliance as opposed to partial compliance
theory."[1] Rawls admitted at once that the problems
of partial compliance, which arise because people
do *not* in fact behave justly, "are the urgent and
pressing matters."[2] Still, he said, "The reason for
beginning with ideal theory is that it provides, I
believe, the only basis for a systematic grasp of these
more pressing problems."[3]

That is the first time the phrase "ideal theory" occurs in his book—and it is not defined there. But a
few pages earlier he *had* defined a well-ordered society more fully as one that is

> not only designed to advance the good of its
> members but . . . also effectively regulated by a
> public conception of justice. That is, it is a so-
> ciety in which (1) everyone accepts and knows
> that the others accept the same principles of
> justice, and (2) the basic social institutions gen-
> erally satisfy and are known to satisfy these
> principles.[4]

So, in the context, he clearly means that an ideal
theory is one that is worked out for a well-ordered
society, whose members and whose institutions are
known by all to meet these two conditions: they

have a shared commitment to an ideal of justice, and their institutions more or less realize it.

What's not immediately obvious is why a theory worked out for a well-ordered society should be helpful in thinking about justice in any actual society, which won't, on reasonable sociopsychological assumptions, be well ordered . . . not the least because of what Rawls called, as we saw, the "urgent and pressing" problems created by unjust behavior. Laura Valentini puts a first problem here clearly:

> To be sure, ideal theory allows us to identify instances of partial compliance (by telling us what full compliance requires), but it does not tell us how to respond to them. . . . To see this, it suffices to consider phenomena such as world poverty. . . . Their persistence is to a large extent due to people's—both ordinary citizens' and officials'—unwillingness to act on the duties that apply to them (e.g., to help the poor . . .). The important question for a political theory aiming at guiding action in the real world, then, is "What ought we to do in circumstances where others do not do their part?"[5]

In a world of partial compliance, a theory concocted for full compliance is not guaranteed to tell us anything very much.[6] Some critics of ideal political theory—notably Charles W. Mills and Elizabeth Anderson—go further. By omitting race- and gender-based structures of subordination, they maintain, Rawls's idealizations can be, in Anderson's words, "epistemologically disabling," effectively blinding us to those forms of injustice.[7]

These objections are similar to ones that have been urged against Robert Nozick's proposal in *Anarchy, State, and Utopia* of what he called an "entitlement theory" of justice. Nozick thought that in a world of full compliance,

> the following inductive definition would exhaustively cover the subject of justice in holdings.
>
> 1. A person who acquires a holding in accordance with the principle of justice in acquisition is entitled to that holding.
>
> 2. A person who acquires a holding in accordance with the principle of justice in transfer, from someone else entitled to the holding, is entitled to the holding.
>
> 3. No one is entitled to a holding except by (repeated) applications of 1 and 2.[8]

But in the actual world of partial compliance, as he himself pointed out,

> Some people steal from others, or defraud them,
> or enslave them, seizing their product and pre-
> venting them from living as they choose, or
> forcibly exclude others from competing in ex-
> changes. . . . And some persons acquire holdings
> by means not sanctioned by the principle of justice
> in acquisition.

So, to deal with the actual world you need to figure
out how to restore justice when such violations
occur. "Idealizing greatly," Nozick wrote, "let us
suppose that theoretical reflection will produce a
principle of rectification. . . . I shall not attempt that
task here."[9]

The challenge, though, is harder than this passage acknowledges: Because almost none of the
property in the world today meets the first two
conditions—having been unjustly acquired or else
unjustly transferred at least once—all the real work
is going to have to be done by the principle of rectification of holdings; and about this our intuitions,
like Nozick's theory, which, as we just saw, was left
for later, are much sketchier than they are about
justice in acquisition and transfer. Even if the
part of the theory that deals with a world in which
people do what they should—the ideal theory—is

well-developed and, perhaps, even plausible, it doesn't help much in the circumstances of an actual non-ideal world. (And, again, the Lockean elements of this account can be charged with distracting readers from the historical patterns of subordination they elide.)[10]

One can imagine similar objections to Ronald Dworkin's use, in *Sovereign Virtue*, of ideas about auctions and insurance to characterize what justice demands for the distribution of goods. Dworkin says there, plausibly enough, that what society owes each of us is an equal initial share of resources, and that then it is fine to let inequalities develop as people apply their different ambitions to producing and exchanging goods and services in the market and in giving and receiving gifts. Because people are different, he acknowledges, it may be hard to say what it is to give them an equal share of the world's bounty. But he has a solution to this problem, involving a once-for-all-times auction—imagined among the new arrivals on a desert island—whose elegant details do not matter for our purposes. When we move from an idealized world, like the island, to the real world, however, we can apply the insights gained there only if there are ways to take account of the differences between idealization and reality. But Dworkin's ideal of equal resources offers no guidance in taking this key step. It is a central fact of our moral lives that we enter history one at a time; Dworkin's auction, on the other hand, only makes sense, as he himself insists, if it happens once and for all. (Even on a desert island something would eventually need to be said about what resources to grant to each new child that came along.)[11]

You can see the problem clearly enough in what seems to be a much simpler case: that of justice for asylum seekers, to which I will turn in a little more detail later. There is disagreement about whether or not in an ideally just world there would be many states. We do not need to decide this issue. Suppose in a just world there would be no states (or, if you prefer, only one). Then there would be no questions about asylum—which, by definition, one state grants to citizens of another—in a just world. So an ideal theory tells us nothing. Now suppose that there would be states in a just world. They would all themselves be just. Then there would be no need for asylum—which, by definition, we grant to those fleeing injustice. So an ideal theory tells us nothing in this case either.

For Rawls, in particular, there is a pressing problem that has to do with the way in which he argued for his principles of justice. They were to be chosen as the best option by contractors in an imaginary "original position." These contractors were to know nothing about when or where or who they would be. But they would otherwise be rather well informed. "They understand political affairs and the principles of economic theory," Rawls wrote. "They know the basis of social organization and the laws of human psychology." But *if* they know these things, won't they design principles that take account of the fact that a society with demanding standards of justice won't be well ordered? Isn't that, after all, one of the truths about human psychology, all of which they know?

Here a defender of Rawls might want to insist that what we need to know in the original position is that full compliance with the principles of justice is possible, not that it is likely. Because what we have is empirical knowledge about the social and psychological world, the "possible" here must mean not logically possible but psychologically possible, possible for people as they are. (I put aside the idealizations represented by Rawls's originally positioned parties, who are more angelic than human: these "deputies of a kind of everlasting moral agent or institution" exemplify a concept of rationality "that is the standard one familiar in social theory," and they are devoid of envy, mutually disinterested, etc.)[12] There is an empirical dispute here to be had, and I confess that while rough conformity to the demands that Rawls makes may be psychologically possible, full compliance strikes me as not something that current social science would suggest is a possibility. Rawls spends time in his book arguing that the institutions of the liberal society he imagines would be stable, given what human beings are like: by which he means that citizens would be broadly compliant with them through time. So his position on this question is not assumed, but argued. But the conclusions he draws suggest only that most normal people raised in such a society might be inclined to comply most of the time. One of the truths we know in the original position is that there will be sociopaths; another is that most of us lapse from virtue at least occasionally.

But in any case, the challenge I want to make to the Rawlsian project is not that its psychology is mistaken (though, on his own account, that *would* be an objection) but to ask why the right way to proceed, in framing the rules of a just society, is to examine the consequences of adopting rules with which people will almost certainly not comply fully. Why not proceed by considering norms whose realization our social science suggests would be likely?

Why, in other words, would people in the original position make a well-ordered society one of their idealizing assumptions? It is question-begging at this point to make the argument Rawls actually makes: that only so can we understand the result that partial compliance deviates from. For him, partial compliance is partial compliance with the principles of justice chosen in the original position. If those principles took account of actual psychology, they could treat defection from Rawls's ideals (to whatever degree that it is inescapable for actual human beings) as permissible—and consider the virtues of a world of full compliance with a rule that was less demanding; and then this behavior would not count as *defection* from the principles thus modified.

But these issues are not just problems for major theorists like Rawls and Nozick and Dworkin. In thinking about principles or practices, it is natural for *anyone* to reflect on the case of full compliance, defending a principle or a practice by arguing that a world in which everyone conformed to the principle or followed the practice would be a fine place. Rule-utilitarians argue that conformity to a certain rule would be utility-maximizing. Most of us agree, whether or not we are utilitarians, that this is an argument in favor of the rule. It is a standard and a natural way to argue. But whether that recommends actually adopting the principle or the practice surely depends not just on what would happen in theory if people conformed to it, but also on whether people are likely in fact to conform to it.[13]

Consider a familiar kind of dispute. One philosopher—let us call her Dr. Welfare—proposes that we should act in a way that maximizes human well-being. What could be more evident than that *this* would make for the best world? Another—Prof. Partiality—proposes instead that we should avoid harm to others in general but focus our benevolence on those to whom we have special ties. There is every reason to doubt that this will make a world in which everyone is as well off as could be. But a world in which everyone is succeeding in complying pretty well with Prof. Partiality's prescription might be better (by standards they share) than a world where most of us are failing pretty miserably to comply with Dr. Welfare's. And given what people are actually like, one might suppose that these are the likely outcomes.

The issue here, then, is about the role of ideals in our moral life. Prof. Partiality could argue that an ideal that is within reach, the pursuit of which might actually make for a better world, is preferable to one so far beyond our capacity that, in aiming for it, we will end up actually doing less good. Notice that this claim is of exactly the same form as the argument we made for cognitive heuristics earlier: aiming lower and succeeding can leave you better off than aiming too high and failing, and those may be the only serious options we face.

Back to Basics

It will help here, I think, to get back to basics and to recall what we learned from Vaihinger in Chapter 1 about the nature of idealization. But let me remind you, first, that I am laying aside the proposal that all normative language is a kind of fiction and that shoulds and oughts are always reflections, not of beliefs, but of affective attitudes. Fictionalism about morality—the claim that moral language involves making-believe that there are moral facts—is another form of as-if philosophy, but (as I said at the start) it raises issues beyond those I have been discussing. For Vaihinger's fundamental thoughts, remember, are two: first, that in idealization we build a picture—a model—of something that proceeds *as if* something we know is false were true; and second, that we do so because the resulting model is useful for some purpose. (At the end of Chapter 2, drawing on Walton, we added that treating something as true means acting as we would if we believed it, but only in some limited contexts and respects.)

Vaihinger suggested, apropos of idealization in the natural sciences, that one purpose guiding idealization might be managing the world; another, he suggested, apropos of theology, might be managing ourselves. The usefulness in each case of the idealization depends upon facts about us, about the world in which we are embedded, and about our relation to that world outside ourselves. In the natural sciences, Vaihinger thought, it is the complexity of the world that makes idealization useful—and that means its complexity-for-us, because different false assumptions might be useful for a creature with greater, or lesser, powers of memory or computation than ours. In theology, on the other hand, Vaihinger thinks, it is the fact that our moral motivations are strengthened by the "poetry" of religious stories that makes creeds useful for us. (This thought, remember, was endorsed by

Richard Braithwaite.) So even Vaihinger would have to concede that in a world of *Star Trek* Vulcans, whose psychology makes such poetry elusive, a different framework would almost certainly be needed.

John Rawls built a model of the just society assuming what is false of the actual world, namely, full compliance with the norms of justice. He said this was useful for acquiring a "systematic grasp" of the urgent problems that arise because people will not, in fact, comply. I have already suggested that this isn't a claim to which, given his method, he is entitled. But Vaihinger's framework allows us to identify the two issues that need to be clarified before we can understand the way idealizations work in political theory, as everywhere else. What false assumptions does this theory presuppose? For what purposes might it be useful to proceed on those false assumptions?

Let's note that idealization in normative theory might proceed in two different ways. One would involve building models in which the false assumptions are themselves not normative. I shall say more about the issues here in a moment. But a second way would be to proceed with models that made false assumptions, not about what *is*, but about what *ought to be* so. To begin with, you might wonder whether one can make sense of this possibility. For what purposes could it be useful to build a model of moral life in which, say, we had no special obligations to our children?[14] Or in which it was a good thing to cause pain to others? I can see that we might want to entertain counter-normatives—counterfactuals whose antecedents are normative propositions that are false—in the course of reasoning about normative questions. But what use could it be to construct theories about what is just or good that are explicitly conditional on untruths about what *should* be so? The question strikes me as one worth exploring further.

Counter-normativity

The prospects for such a theory will depend on what kind of usefulness you have in mind. I was assuming just now that the question was whether such theories—let me dub them *counter-normative*—might be useful for understanding some features of our moral situation, as I claimed decision theory was useful for understanding some features of our cognitive situation. For a counter-normative theory of this sort to be useful in understanding would be for us to learn something by, so to speak, acting-in-thought in some of the ways we would if—contrary to fact—it were true. But for Vaihinger the question is whether acting in certain respects and in certain contexts as if such a theory were true allows us to control some aspects of the world.

So what is it for a normative theory to help us control the world? One possibility is that it makes us more likely to succeed in our dealings with other people in a way that makes the world better. How, though, can we judge a theory's contribution to making the world better without already having an account of what it is for the world to *be* better? Won't asking this question about a moral theory, M, require us already to have an answer to the very questions that M aims to answer? Well, no, as we have seen already with Dr. Welfare. For Dr. Welfare can agree that, if we human beings with our limited capacities for sympathy are to make the world better by her standards, it will be better if we act for the most part as if Professor Partiality were right. Professor Partiality's theory, she can say, is better than hers for action: Generally, we should act as if his view were true, although in the realm of theoretical reflection we should be clear that he is wrong.

The situation here seems to me parallel to the one with decision theory. It sets a standard by which we can see that we, with our limited capacities, should not aim directly at that very standard.[15] There are simpler cases to notice here. Most people who have thought about it conclude that it is false that it is always wrong to lie. But someone might think that, for most ordinary purposes, it will be best to act as if "Lying is wrong" were true.[16] And to act as if it were true is not just to try to avoid lying, but also to feel guilty when one lies, to avoid liars, to urge the avoidance of lies upon one's children, and so on. This will mean that even in the cases where one realizes it is right to lie and does so, one may feel guilty. The same is true, I think, about "Torture is wrong." Perhaps one can conceive of sufficiently strange and unfortunate circumstances in which, all things considered, one is not just free to torture another person but one is actually required to do so—if (in the sort of case that torture-enthusiasts routinely trot out) the choice was between torturing this one person and permitting the deaths of hundreds, say. But even if that is theoretically the case, it will be better if what I carry around in my head and act on is the thought that torture is wrong. This is not just because in most likely circumstances torture actually *would* be wrong. Carrying in my head a more complex or more hedged claim would require me to check even the easy cases against a complicated rule, wasting time that could be better spent doing other things. Worse, carrying the hedged rule about might actually leave me more likely to commit torture when I clearly shouldn't. In "Modern Moral Philosophy," Elizabeth Anscombe announced that the prohibition on murdering the innocent was absolute, and that the "strictness of the prohibition has as its point that you are not to be tempted by fear or hope of consequences."[17] Perhaps, you could think, a world at peace in which I believed that it was always wrong to murder the innocent would be one in which I almost always did what I should, whereas in a world in which I weighed the consequences of acting on that belief I might end up being tempted to murder.

We should distinguish here between two different questions. One is a question I can ask myself. Should I act as if murder is absolutely wrong, no exceptions considered? I can conclude that even though it isn't true, this principle is worth acting on; and I might especially think this after undertaking theoretical reflection and imaginative exploration that convince me that it is remarkably unlikely that I will ever be in one of those situations where it might be that murder was permissible (and even less likely that I will ever be in one where it is required). Here we are following Vaihinger.

But we can also ask whether it would be better not if *I* did so, but if *we* did so. Consider a world in which almost everyone acted as if killing the innocent was absolutely wrong. Suppose that this is false, because you could reasonably believe that a person who is in fact innocent is trying to murder you, and that in such a case killing him or her would not be wrong. Still, in such a world, *that* circumstance is extremely unlikely to arise. Here is one of the reasons it might be useful for us to act as if something is so: because the world will be better if all or most of us act as if it is so. On the other hand, if I alone acted as if murder were always wrong in a world of people who took it to be false, it might not be something that it was useful for me to believe at all.

There is another important feature of this case. The results may be better if people act as if murder is exceptionlessly wrong, *whether or not they know that this is, strictly speaking, false.* Vaihinger wasn't interested in cases where we profited from acting as if something that was actually false was true, even though we didn't know it was false. For him, idealization is something that you know you are doing. I shall follow him in considering only the cases where the falsehood in question is understood, to some degree, to be a falsehood worth proceeding with. (So we are not in the ambit of a Platonic "noble lie.") But I shall not follow him in being interested only in the question whether something is useful for me—or some single person—to believe but will rather consider, too, the more general question of whether it can be useful for *us* to agree to act as if something we know to be false is true.

Questions like how we should record our attitudes to lying and torture and murder—whether we should act as if they are always wrong—might receive a different answer in the singular and in the plural. And one reason is that there are beliefs whose widespread acceptance can help make them closer to true. An obvious example here, discussed by Philip Pettit under the rubric of the "cunning of trust," is the normative belief that people ought to be trusted.[18] This is not something to go by in a society where most people don't believe it. In such a society, he points out, people will misrecognize overtures of trust; they may also feel free to take advantage of trusting people because they are saps, doing something most people think imprudent. But perhaps in a world where most people do believe you should trust other people, most people should in fact be trusted. Even in that world it isn't going to be absolutely true: but the more people believe it, the more often the world will go the way we want it to. It will always be an idealization, but it will, in a certain obvious sense, be less of an idealization, the more people act as if it is true.[19]

I have proceeded on the assumption that what these moral theories are useful for is making the world better. Most of us will want to consider them for that purpose, because most of us do want to make the world better, even if we aren't always clear about how that is to be done.

But you could find it useful to act as if a certain false moral claim were true in ways that allowed you to control the social world in pursuit of immoral aims. This is not just a conceptual possibility. Suppose there are people who know that certain moral claims are true (I shouldn't cause pain to innocent creatures) but who are also inclined generally to act as if they are not (I get a kick from torturing this cat); and, furthermore, they think that the world goes better for them because they do this (I don't see what good it does *me* to do what is right). So they are controlling the world by acting on a belief—it's okay to cause pain to innocent creatures—that they know to be false. That fits the description offered by moral psychologists of some psychopaths. I think it would be odd to call what they are doing idealizing; but the oddity is only that idealizing is ordinarily thought of in a positive light. These people are taking up an option that fits Vaihinger's framework. They are acting as if something they concede to be false is true, because that helps them control their social world, in the sense of having it go the way they would like it to go.

No doubt much more needs to be said here. We would need, for example, to explore the long-standing dispute in moral theory between internalists, who hold that you can only sincerely hold that you ought to do something if you are motivated by that thought toward doing it, and externalists, who hold that you can know something is right while not being motivated toward doing it at all. (Internalists don't think that you must actually try to do it; other things can get in the way of the motivation.) If you were such a moral internalist, you could think that knowing what's right motivates you to do it, and that someone who does what is in fact right for external reasons—reasons that have nothing to do with its being right—is not acting as if it is right at all. Most people would say that the crook or psychopath isn't acting as if stealing is wrong; he's acting as if stealing is permissible, but is sanctioned and discouraged, so that he must conceal his actions. The point is that, in deciding whether someone is acting as if it were true that *p*, we are asking whether they are acting as they would if they believed that *p*: and so we need an account of what it is to have a moral belief before we can apply the notion of acting as if a moral claim is true.

Hacking's Loops: Pretending to Believe in Identities

Counter-normatives reflect a neglected form of as-if thinking in ethical thought. Like each of the major topics I discuss in this book, I think they deserve more consideration. I hope I have done enough to support that claim. But I want to turn now to a form of as-if thinking in normative theory that has received a good deal more attention. This is the kind of model building in moral and political theory that assumes away features of our actual psychological or social lives, in the manner that Adam Smith did in the work that Vaihinger discussed.

Here it is factual rather than normative untruths that play into our theorizing, as they do, in ways I have pointed out already, in the work of Rawls, Nozick, and Dworkin.

Let me begin here with a kind of idealization that builds moral theories about groups whose existence the theorist, strictly speaking, denies. Many moral claims seem to be about just such groups. In earlier work of my own, for example, I have argued both that races, strictly speaking, don't exist, and that it is wrong to discriminate on the basis of a person's race. This can usually be parsed out in a way that is not strictly inconsistent: What is wrong is discrimination against someone because you believe her to be, say, a Negro even though there are, in fact, strictly speaking, no Negroes. But in responding to discrimination with affirmative action, we find ourselves assigning people to racial categories. We think it justified to treat people as if they had races even when we officially believe that they don't. What is going on in cases like this?

Part of what happens here is a consequence of the way that mistaken beliefs can generate social categories, despite their being mistaken. Ian Hacking has pointed to the ways in which scientific theories that invoke categories of persons—homosexuals, individuals with dissociative identity disorder—interact with the behavior of people who are so labeled, of doctors, and of everyone else to produce what he calls "looping effects."

> We think of many kinds of people as objects of scientific inquiry. Sometimes to control them, as prostitutes, sometimes to help them, as potential suicides. Sometimes to organize and help, but at the same time keep ourselves safe, as the poor or the homeless. Sometimes to change them for their own good and the good of the public, as the obese. Sometimes just to admire, to understand, to encourage and perhaps even to emulate, as (sometimes) geniuses. We think of these kinds of people as definite classes defined by definite properties. As we get to know more about these properties, we will be able to control, help, change, or emulate them better. But it's not quite like that. They are moving targets because our investigations interact with them, and change them. And since they are changed, they are not quite the same kind of people as before. The target has moved. I call this the "looping effect." Sometimes, our sciences create kinds of people that in a certain sense did not exist before. I call this "making up people."[20]

The most obvious example of this is one given prominence in the work of Michel Foucault. It may be that in England in the late nineteenth century a Vaihingerian sexologist could have commended acting as if there were basically just homosexuals (a kind of person whose sexuality is naturally constituted so that they have erotic attractions exclusively to their own sex) and heterosexuals (a kind of person whose sexuality is naturally constituted so that they have erotic attractions exclusively to the other sex).[21] Perhaps, he might have added, there are some bisexuals, subject to both attractions, and asexuals subject to none, too. This belief could have been useful for men who found themselves with attractions to men, even if there really were no such kinds of person then. "Sexuality," the Vaihingerian sexologist could have said to them, "is actually quite fluid and complex and everyone has a sexuality whose erotic objects are defined by more than gender; there are also many men who are erotically engaged with men some of the time but not always, and, certainly not with every sort of man. (*Mutatis mutandis*, so too for women.) But, *for practical purposes*, think of yourself as a homosexual. That will allow you best to manage your social and erotic world."[22]

In fact what happened historically was not that people took this idea up as a fiction: they took it up as a hypothesis. And through the looping effects of theories of sexuality, both scientific and popular, people came to act as homosexuals because that is what they believed they were. Theories about what that meant, again both scientific and popular, played a role in shaping those beliefs. Some people—Michel Foucault, notoriously—have concluded that this process has resulted in there now being homosexuals, where once there were none. Everyone in the North Atlantic world now either is or isn't a homosexual. A false hypothesis has become true, just as the false hypothesis that people are trustworthy can become true in a society where enough people believe it.

But it would nevertheless be possible for a belief in homosexuality as a category—in gay people and lesbians as kinds of people—to be taken up by someone no longer as a hypothesis but as a fiction (just as Vaihinger's Protestantism began as hypothesis and ended as fiction, too). Nobody is, strictly speaking, gay or straight or bisexual, someone might think, but for the purposes of most standard social interactions nothing much goes wrong if you just *behave* as if everyone is gay or straight or bisexual.

Think of homo-, hetero-, and bi- sexualities as useful fictions.

Simply believing that there really are or really aren't any homosexuals is not yet to have a moral belief. But this form of looping creation of kinds of person—kinds that can work either as hypothesis or as fiction—is certainly relevant to moral life. Once you have identities like these, they figure in moral claims. That it is not wrong to be homosexual is one of the moral claims of the Roman Catholic Church. (This belief is combined with the belief that homoerotic acts—which our sexologist thought were the "natural expression" of homosexuality—*are* nevertheless wrong.) A rigorous Catholic thinker might say, "Look, strictly speaking nobody is a homosexual. But for practical purposes it's too complicated to say what people actually are. Indeed, we have no theories that adequately capture the truths about the kinds of human sexuality." Our rigorous Catholic could construct a moral account of sexuality that was an idealization because it proceeded as if there really were homosexuals, heterosexuals, bisexuals, and so on, though in fact he accepted (*in pectore*, as he might say) that there were not.

I have mentioned dissociative identity disorder and sexuality. But Hacking's loops can be present in almost any kind of social identity; so ultimately this discussion is about considering a society filled with people of various identities, which means—because, as Joseph de Maistre rightly insisted, there is "no such thing as a man," uninflected by identities— every society.[23] In every society, there will be identities; and their shape will often be the result of people acting as if things that are not strictly speaking true are in fact true. That is surely the situation with "race" in much of the modern world: educated people know that many of the biological and psychological assumptions presupposed in much talk of race are false (so there are, *sensu stricto*, no races), but they behave in many contexts as if this were not so.

Identities, conceived of as stable features of a social ontology grounded in natural facts, are often, then, assumed in our moral thinking, even though, in our theoretical hearts, we know them not to be real. They are one of our most potent idealizations.

What Should We Take for Granted?

But we need to step back for a moment and think about whether there are facts about the human world we should *not* assume away in our moral reflection. This is not an easy question. For there is a deep problem for thinking about idealization in normative theory that is a consequence of the fact that theory here aims to identify not how things are but how things should be—what we should do and feel and be, what would make for a better, juster world. Reflection on those questions must presumably take account of some facts. *Ought*, after all, usually implies *can*. But *is* certainly doesn't imply *ought*. And the fact that something isn't so does not, by itself, rule out the possibility that it should be. So moral theory starts with a view of how people are while also having a view about how they should be, and knowing that the former is far from the latter.

Consider again my rigorous Catholic moralist. He might take a different tack. "Perhaps," he might say, "Michel Foucault is right and homosexuals came into being as a kind as a result of the historical processes he described. This is actually something we should regret, since it would be better if there were no homosexuals in this sense. (Not in the sense that it would be better if these people didn't exist or that they should be wiped out, but in the sense that these very people could have existed without being homosexual, if these looping effects had not occurred.) They might still have had the occasional stray desire for sex with another man but they wouldn't have thought that this defined them as a kind of person; as, indeed, many people in the human past had such desires but did not think that gave them an identity. Our Church teaches that almost everyone has sexual desires they ought not to act on: parish priests, bishops, and cardinals, if they are honest, confess such desires all the time. It seems unhelpful, in this case, to organize a social identity around an illicit desire.[24] Perhaps there are people who cannot have satisfactory heteroerotic encounters for a great variety of reasons, of which this is only one. We should find caring ways to deal with this fact, but organizing people to think that they have identities as homosexuals or asexuals or, God forbid, pedophiles is not the answer."[25] He might, that is, take for granted that there are people with these sexualities, but prefer to construct his moral theory for a world in which there weren't, precisely because he believed this counterfactual world would be better. So we can always ask, "Which of the ways we currently are can we reasonably try to aim to escape?"

Well, it is hard to see how you could get going with moral reflection at all if you didn't acknowledge that we are susceptible to pleasure and pain, can experience joy, and are sociable and playful; that we need adequate nutrition, that most of us have sexual desires. I take it that facts like these are the grounds on which we suppose, for example, that people have rights against torture, to sexual privacy and freedom of association, to food, water, and a place to live. A morality for creatures without pain and joy and affection and sexual desire, who took no pleasure in make-believe, who did not need food or water or shelter, would presumably be different from the morality we actually have. And it would in any case be rather unhelpful in thinking about life for *Homo sapiens*.

I don't mean to deny that we could imagine a world in which there were no sexual desires of any kind. In that world, if we wanted the species to continue, we would have to make new arrangements to produce new people. That would make some things more complicated, but many other things would also be simpler, no doubt. Still, you might ask, what purpose would be served by idealizing sexuality away? Well, we might want to ask what the world might be like without sex and eros and if that world might be better. Suppose such reflection persuaded us that it *would* be better. Would we then be bound to see the fact of sex and sexuality as regrettable, as something that we might aim to eradicate by trying to produce people who do not have sexual desires, and to develop artificial means of reproducing the species? To conclude that there is a reason to disfavor such a world because we, as we now are, would not take to it, is perhaps no more reasonable than the child's argument in saying, "I'm glad I hate peas, because if I liked them I'd eat them . . . and I hate them."

I do not care for the thought of a world without eros. But there are features of our nature that it would be much more tempting to lay aside. Almost all of us are also prone to envy, cruelty, and malice. Should our normative theorizing take these, too, as given? And what does it mean to take them as given? We can certainly take them as given in the sense of proposing principles and institutions that respond to the urgent problems created by these vices. We can take them as given by dealing with them in non-ideal theory, the theory of partial compliance. But if we took them as given in the sense of supposing that there was no point in recommending against them, then we would be left with a morality in which whatever is, is right; and that would, in fact, be a world without morality at all. The point, then, is that some aspects of human nature have to be taken as given in normative theorizing in this second sense, but to take us exactly as we are would involve giving up ideals altogether. So when should we ignore, and when insist on, human nature?

Staying in Character

There is a recent dispute about what facts we should take into account in constructing not political but moral theory that will prove instructive: it is the attack—in the name of situationist psychology—on virtue ethics. On one standard recent view, a virtuous act is one that a virtuous person would do, done for the reasons a virtuous person would do it. Character is primary; virtues are more than simple dispositions to do the right thing. As Daniel C. Russell says, "Virtue ethics tells us that what is right is to be a certain kind of person, a person of virtue." Such a person will express his or her virtue through actions, but rules of right action are "largely a secondary matter," because the virtues are character traits.[26] Those who draw on Aristotle's ideas are likely to stress, with Rosalind Hursthouse, that the dispositions in question are deep, stable, and enmeshed in yet other traits and dispositions; honesty, for instance, "goes all the way down," and spreads broadly across a range of emotions, reactions, attitudes, and interests.[27] The virtues, in sum, are what we need in order to flourish, to have what Aristotle called *eudaimonia*: a virtuous character is one that will allow us to live well. The task of ethics, then, will be to discover what traits of character we need to live well, and work back from there.

But just as modern moral philosophers were rediscovering the virtues, social psychologists were uncovering evidence that most actual people (including people ordinarily thought to be, say, honest) don't exhibit virtues of this stable, broad-spectrum variety. (The claim, to be clear from the start, is not the absurd one that we have no dispositions at all; it is that we don't have the *right* sort of dispositions.) These psychologists were advancing a "situationist" account, which emphasizes systematic human tendencies to respond to features of their situations that nobody previously thought to be crucial at all.[28] They think that someone who is, say, reliably honest in one kind of situation will often be reliably dishonest in another. They'd predict that Oskar Schindler could be a bundle of characterological contradictions; that his courage and compassion could be elicited in some contexts but not in others.[29]

Let us suppose for the moment that the situation-ists are roughly right about the virtues. (I should say that many virtue ethicists simply don't believe this.) The virtue ethicists can still declare themselves to be engaging in idealization. Indeed, they might say, the picture of the virtues was always explicitly conceived of as an ideal: something hard to strive for, impossible, perhaps, to achieve, but still worth aiming at. We might be at a simple standoff here if we didn't have Vaihinger's second question to take us further: For what purposes is this idealization supposed to be useful?

We cannot answer this question, I think, without first asking what, more precisely, the psychologists are claiming. That people don't exhibit the virtues threatens no claim of the virtue ethicist, because the theory is about what should be, not about what is. So, to be relevant, the psychological claims have to be to some degree modal: They have to be not just about our current natures but also about our ca-pabilities. They have to be saying that many or most or all of us *could* not develop the virtues, un-derstood in this way.

Given the gradually expanding knowledge we have of psychology and neuroscience, it seems to me far from evident that our current incapacity to develop the virtues guarantees that we *couldn't* produce them eventually, by neural reprogramming or genetic manipulation. And if, in the end, we *don't*, I suspect it will be because we think that it would be wrong to interfere with people in the necessary ways, not because it is literally impossible to do so. Ronald Dworkin rightly insisted—and here, as he said, he was following Aristotle—that the value of human lives comes from the challenge of working with our socially developed natures; substituting different natures artificially might amount to a kind of cheating.[30] So that the modal truth here—that we *can't* develop the virtues—may actually itself be normative rather than natural. It might be that what we really think is that we shouldn't do so. But once more let us concede *arguendo* the claim that virtue is often unachievable.

Could it still be useful to characterize the virtues even if there were no possibility that most of us could actually develop them? Might the situation here be like the situation that I suggested for decision theory: that we were characterizing a kind of moral life— that of the virtuous agent—and at the same time recognizing that it was not possible for us?

In the case of decision theory, the discovery that the rationality of the computationally perfect agent was not possible for us led us to recommend strategies, heuristics, that would get us closer, in our actual situations, to the outcomes that would occur if we aimed directly to implement the ideal. But here there is a disanalogy. For the virtues are conceived of as worthwhile, not just because of what they lead us to do, but because of the kind of people that virtuous agents are. And the analog of a heuristic here would presumably be the development of the capacity to do, in many normal circumstances, what the honest person would *do* . . . without actually *being* honest. And to accept *that* instead would be to give up a critical tenet of virtue theory, which is, as I say, that there are things that it is important to be and to feel as well as things that it is important to do. So if the situationists were right, there would indeed be some reason to abandon the ideal of virtue as a way of being.

That would still leave open a different kind of view, according to which what matters about the virtues is strictly how they lead us to behave. Discovering ways of behaving honestly that are not themselves the result of an honest character could then be worth pursuing, even if the situationists were right.[31] Mark Alfano has added an interesting wrinkle of complexity to the question whether talk about character could be useful even if the situationists were right. In his *Character as Moral Fiction* he argues that believing in character can make people behave in ways that are closer to the ways a virtuous person would behave. As he puts it, apropos of the intellectual virtues of curiosity and industry: "People who are not yet curious start to act curiously when they are called curious. People who are not yet academically sedulous begin to work hard in school when they are labeled as hardworking." In short, "the tactical use of certain fictions leads to *factitious intellectual virtues*."[32] There are echoes here of Vaihinger's thought that theological fictions—religious myths—can be tactically mobilized to shape behavior in useful ways even though they are known not to be true.

Back to Politics

These questions about how much of human nature should be taken for granted in moral theory—that is, as not up for revision or reform—are difficult. But idealization in *political* theory strikes me as somewhat more tractable, for a simple reason: it has generally been, in one way, more explicit. In political theory, we often take a basic ethical picture—a picture of the good life for human beings—as given and ask what consequences it has for the proper organization of our public life. And usually the moral psychology presupposed is laid out more or less explicitly and the norms of public life are defended as making for a good life for people with that moral psychology. The pictures are famously various: Hobbes's fearful rational egoist, Smith's more sympathetic but also self-interested economic man, Bentham's utility consumer, Tocqueville's man of honor, Rawls's self-respecting person with her moral powers, sense of justice, and conception of the good, Nussbaum and Sen's men and women with their capabilities. But all of them are understood as ideal types, not precise descriptions. At the very least, they aim to leave out some facts about what we are like and to simplify—that is idealize and thus misrepresent—the complex truths about our human lives. This is defensible, in the first place, for the reason that Vaihinger said that idealization in economics was defensible: the world is too complex for us to take it all into account. And precisely for this reason it can be useful to work with pictures that idealize in many distinct ways.

In the case of our theory of mind (and the intentional strategy of Dennett's that went with it), we noticed that we needed an account of what we were like that was richer than the one presupposed in our idealization, in order to assess the claim that we have good reason to ignore facts about our situation. I suggested that we didn't have such an account. But in political theory, evaluating this claim is possible, because we have quite rich and well-supported psychological theories that we know we are leaving out of account in the picture of the human person as political agent we work with; and we can consider, case by case, whether adding something we know to our picture would enrich our theorizing in ways that are helpful. When Richard Thaler and Cass Sunstein claim in *Nudge* that current psychology does indeed have implications for what we should do, that is what they are up to.[33] And Adam Smith's use, some of the time, of a much more austere psychology—the rational egoism of his economic theory—was, as Vaihinger and Buckle insisted, a paradigm of useful idealization.

In fact, disputes about whether some political theories take too much or too little of the facts about people or the world into account are extremely familiar. We regularly hear people object to theories as "utopian," where what this means is that their

realization would require changes in human behavior or attitude that we are unlikely to be able—or
simply have no idea how—to bring about. And on
the other hand, we hear objections that suggest that
a political theory takes too much of the world as
given, that it is cynical: that it doesn't, in effect, idealize enough.

Much political theory until recent times, for
example, took for granted the existence of national
boundaries and discussed questions about issues
like the rights of asylum I mentioned earlier, assuming that states with boundaries would always
be a feature of the world. But as I observed there,
you might object to such proposals that if the issue
is justice, we cannot assume that it is just that there
are national boundaries at all. Questions about
justice in migration, some people think, ought to
be discussed without assuming the system of
nation-states.

In adjudicating this dispute, wisdom lies, I think,
in remembering once more the second of Vaihinger's
questions: not "What facts are you assuming away?"
but "For what purposes is the assumption useful?"
As Joseph Carens has rightly pointed out in discussing "Realistic and Idealistic Approaches to the
Ethics of Migration," the idealizations that are

useful for one purpose may not be useful for another.[34] I am going to explore Carens's discussion briefly now: it will enable us to see some of the issues for idealization in political theory a little more clearly.

Theories of Migration

Carens aims to address the ethics of migration. And he begins by identifying two different approaches that have been adopted in the literature on the topic, which he labels "realistic" and "idealistic." He writes, "The former is especially attentive to the constraints that must be accepted if morality is to serve as an effective guide to action in the world in which we currently live. The latter is especially concerned with issues of fundamental justification and inclined to challenge what is in the name of what is right."[35] And he cites the great political theorist Stanley Hoffman, who wrote in defense of his own realist approach in his book *Duties beyond Borders*:

> One of the key necessities in this field is to avoid too big a gap between what is and what ought to be. In any system of law, or in any system of morals,

there is always a gap between the *is* and the *ought*, between the empirical pattern and the norm. The gap is necessary and inevitable. If there were no gap, people would not feel any sense of obligation, or any remorse when they violate a norm. But when the gap becomes too big, the system of law or the system of morals is really doomed—to have no impact whatsoever or to be destroyed.[36]

Notice that Hoffman is rejecting theories that idealize too heavily (or too lightly) precisely because they won't be useful for the purpose for which political theory of his kind exists: namely, in guiding and in motivating actual political behavior. He is, in effect, accepting Vaihinger's framing of the issues and defending his preferred approach in the light of it.

What Carens does next is to identify the sorts of facts about the world that a realist of this sort might be unwilling to idealize away: he dubs them "institutional, behavioral and political." His example of an institutional fact is the very modern state that I mentioned earlier. "From a realistic perspective, whatever we might want to say about migration should accept as a starting point the division of the world into states that are, at least formally, sovereign and independent."[37] For a behavioral fact he gives the tendency of states to limit their willingness to accept refugees. "The United States and Canada accept many more (in relation to population) than most states. They are proud of their records in this area. From the perspective of a realistic morality, their pride is justifiable because they do more than other countries. They deserve praise and admiration for their policies. It would be pointless to ask whether they do their fair share. . . . It would be even more senseless to criticize these two nations for failing to live up to some abstract standard, like admitting all refugees who want to come."[38] Finally, among political facts, he mentions "who gains and who loses from different migration policies and what resources various actors can bring to bear in a conflict over migration issues."[39]

The thought here is that one kind of political theory refuses to idealize away such facts, because to do so would make theory useless as a guide for actual policy making. If that is right, then there is always a possible criticism here of the approach, namely, that it misjudges what policies are actually achievable; that it takes as given, things—like the currently limited sympathy of people in the admitting states—that could in fact be changed. Taking institutional, behavioral, and political facts such as these for granted could exclude what are in fact real possibilities.

For these real possibilities to be visible, then, you need a more idealistic approach, in Carens's use of that term, one that considers what would be desirable in a world in which there were no national borders, or fewer limitations of sympathy, or different political resources for change. So there is a place, on this view, for a range of kinds of political theory that are idealizing to different degrees. Some, that is, will treat more falsehoods as true than others. And there is an empirical dimension of argument about the adequacy of the more realistic policy proposals that has to do with hypotheses in political psychology and sociology about how fixed the tendencies currently on display actually are. So Carens considers empirical hypotheses in this area. Perhaps, he says, "from a sociological perspective, morality may work best when it fits with long-term or collective interests, even if it conflicts with narrow or self-interested ones." Or perhaps, he suggests, following Sidgwick,

> an ideal morality that has no impact on how people actually behave has no good consequences.

Hence, from a utilitarian perspective, it is not a good morality. If a morality is to be effective, it must be accepted. Hence, in moral argument, we must start with the prevailing moral views and seek no more than incremental changes.[40]

You could object that what Carens is discussing here is not really a matter of two different approaches to *morality*. There's only one morally correct answer to the question how refugees should be treated. It's the one that is visible on what he calls the most idealist theory, one that takes no account of the current institutional, behavioral, and political realities. The realist, on this view, is just someone who accepts an unjust answer that is better than the status quo because she judges that it's the best deal on offer. She seeks what Carens calls incremental changes because she makes a judgment, an empirical, and contestable judgment, about what is achievable sometime soon—about what is, therefore, worth actually trying to realize. This is a perfectly reasonable approach to policy, but it is not an approach to morality at all.

I have some sympathy with this line of criticism. Still, the fact that the more realist approach isn't really answering the moral question—How should refugees be treated, ignoring limitations of sympathy and the like?—doesn't mean it isn't answering any question at all. And one task of political theory is exactly the one the realist identifies. But precisely because it is explicitly motivated by a desire to construct proposals that are feasible now, we can always ask, with Vaihinger's second question in mind: Is it in fact the most useful sort of idealization *for this very purpose?*

I have argued, in my book *The Ethics of Identity,* that aiming for a world without states is not so much infeasible as undesirable: in my view, national partiality is not only politically inevitable but also ethically defensible, because, among other things, the existence of many separate states limits the dangers of unlimited power. So the fact that actual states are unjust, in ways that make seeking asylum a reasonable choice for many, requires us to ask what our own state and others aiming at justice should do for them. And I think the answer is actually quite straightforward: We should accept, if we can—and we *can*—our fair share of those who need to escape, accept more if we are willing and others are not, encourage other states to do the same, and work for a world in which asylum is less necessary. That answer accepts that in a world of partial compliance it is a virtue to do more than we must, precisely because others do less than they should. This is a claim in non-ideal theory, which has at least this to say for it: Compliance with it is possible (Canada and Sweden may well be in compliance already) and makes the world a better place for the victims of injustice.

But it depends, in the end, on a general answer that I favor to a central question of justice we face in a world of partial compliance, a question that ideal theory would never even have to consider. What should we do when we are already doing our fair share and others are not, and, as a result, some are not getting their due? I think we settle what is our fair share by asking for a practice that is possible, and full compliance with which would give everyone his or her due. If there are many practices that would serve, I think we should pick the one that does the most good now and try to get it widely accepted. And then, in the world of noncompliance, it will always be a good thing to do more good than this ourselves; and we must also do our fair share to bring others into compliance.[41]

In deciding whether a practice is possible—which we *must*, in order to apply this idea—we can take people more or less as they are or imagine what would be possible if they were more benevolent, more generous, more virtuous than they are. The more counterfactually virtuous we take people to be, the more idealizing the theory. And there will almost certainly be, for this reason, a range of different answers as to what our fair share is. The most idealized may be useful when we are trying to get ourselves to do more; but a theory that is too idealized may backfire, leading us to conclude that it is not worth trying, so that the best is the enemy of the good. Vaihinger's question—What are we idealizing for?—turns out, once more, to be a useful one.

The Best Is the Enemy of the Better

Rawls set out, as he said, to develop a theory of justice as fairness. Take away the apparatus of the original position, and his basic argument about distributive justice seems to me to be this: A social system is a scheme of cooperation, and in order to be entitled to the support of all its members it must offer each person a satisfactory answer to the question why the advantages it grants to some others it denies to him or her. (That someone rejects such an answer doesn't mean that it isn't satisfactory, in the relevant sense. We have to ask whether this rejection is reasonable.) Rawls's answer, when it came to economic inequality, was that you could justify it if you could show that no one would be better off if we reduced the inequalities, because differential rewards were necessary to incentivize people to create the wealth that a society shares. You could say to the worst off, Rawls thought: "If we took money from the rich, they'd work less hard, and we'd actually be less able to secure your welfare."

But this presupposes that people have the motivational structures that they do. It takes as given a fact about human beings, a fact that a theorist might think it better to idealize away. Perhaps it would be better, that is, to build a theory that started from what a society would be like if people were inclined to work hard because of the intrinsic satisfactions of useful work rather than mostly because of the extrinsic rewards of labor. You might start, then, from the thought that we ought all to work hard to contribute to the social good without differential monetary incentives. One of the reasons people actually work hard is to get more money to afford positional goods—not just a big house but a bigger house than their neighbor's—so that they are motivated by what Hobbes called the "desire for glory," a motivation that they should not have. You might think that the worst off could say: "It's true that rich people wouldn't do the work that generates the wealth we share if we paid them less, but that's because they're insufficiently public spirited. So we—the worst off—*could* be better off if the rich were poorer, provided the rich were willing, as they should be, to do the same work for less." The point is that we have here one of those situations where the question I raised earlier arises: Which of the facts about human beings as we currently are should be taken for granted in political theorizing?[42] And the motivational structure that Rawls assumes can itself be up for moral criticism. So we could refuse to idealize in the way Rawls does, because doing so covers over exactly what is wrong. A committed Rawlsian, Jerry Cohen argued, should be willing to be productive without the incentive of extra pay: Rawls may not be idealizing enough.[43]

I'm not aiming to draw a conclusion about whether Rawls was right about what was fair. Perhaps he was; and perhaps there are reasons to take these motivational structures as given. My point is that reconceiving Rawls's fundamental argument for his difference principle in this way allows us to notice that what's persuasive in the argument doesn't really proceed as he claimed. He presents himself as arguing for an ideal, one that we can then use to test our actual non-ideal society. But the argument I just imagined someone offering—that the rich should take less because they ought to want to work for the common good—doesn't require us to have any view of what things would be like overall in an ideal society. It requires only, as Amartya Sen has argued, that we can compare our current situation in imagination with a different situation and judge one of them better.[44] We start not with a picture of an ideal society but with a question we think anyone can ask about our actual society. "Why am I not getting more of the goods?" And we think that a successful defense of the current distribution would have to show that it was not unfair; or, if it is unfair, unfair in ways that are not remediable at an acceptable cost. (I am skeptical that, in the current world, such a successful defense is possible.)

There's reason to doubt that we have any idea what a perfect society would look like. But we do know that a society in which institutions systematically disadvantage blacks or women or LGBT people is inferior, *for that very reason*, to one that doesn't. Amartya Sen's point is that it is just a mistake to start from a picture of an ideally just society, not because it idealizes too much, taking too many falsehoods as true, but because it misunderstands the epistemology of our moral knowledge about politics. The general point is that you can judge social option A as being better than social option B without starting with a view of the best society and asking whether having A or having B brings you closer to it.

I think this point is a deep and important one. And it is a further argument against conceiving of ideal theory, as Rawls did, as necessarily the right starting point. Often we would do best to start, I think, with what we are best equipped to start with: and that is the comparative judgment that one option is better than another, not an image of what would be best over all.[45]

We should combine this insight with another. The history of our collective moral learning doesn't start with the growing acceptance of a picture of an ideal society. It starts with the rejection of some current actual practice or structure, which we come to see as wrong. You learn to be in favor of equality by noticing what is wrong with the unequal treatment of blacks, or women, or working-class or lower-caste people. You learn to be in favor of freedom by seeing what is wrong in the life of the enslaved or of women in purdah.[46]

In thinking about these sorts of oppression, one conceives of them in an idealizing way, as usual: that is, using a picture that one is aware leaves much out, in order to make the issues graspable. Idealization is necessary here, too, then. But one doesn't need an ideal theory, which starts from a picture of the world as it ought to be. And so, in particular, one doesn't need to start always from thinking about a case where everyone is in full compliance with all the moral demands. Indeed, a reliable picture of that sort is extremely hard to imagine.

But as we've just seen, theories that are non-ideal in Rawls's sense will still idealize in Vaihinger's sense. Even a theory that aims to start, not from where we would ideally be, but from where we actually are, will have to use a picture of where we actually are that idealizes.

Concluding Unscientific Postscript

In these pages we have voyaged over a wide sea of idealizations: in physics and the philosophy of mind, in decision theory, in fiction, in ethics, political philosophy, and political theory. My aim, as I said at the start, has been to commend idealization to you as a topic of reflection and research in all the major areas of the subject. I have been guided by Vaihinger's thought that an idealization involves ignoring the truth in a way that is useful for some purpose; and I have pointed out a great diversity of purposes for which it might be useful. In every case, it is worth asking, I think, whether we can identify the falsehoods we are treating as true, why it might be useful to proceed despite their falsity, and for which purposes it is useful. In the discussion of Dennett's intentional strategy, we saw that we may find ourselves proceeding with what we know is an idealization, while not being able to answer all these questions. But we also saw that, sometimes, as in the case of the idealizations behind one standard account of degrees of belief, answering them can help us see what the theory is—and is not—good for. In this chapter, we've looked at some ways in which idealization in ethics and political philosophy can be motivated and justified; here, too, I think Vaihinger's picture helps us to frame the right questions, even if we cannot always answer them. Part of the reason, as we saw, is that the questions are often complex, empirical social scientific questions about human possibility: What changes in attitude is it feasible to bring about, given the way people are psychologically, given the social structures in which they are embedded?

But in all these domains, in taking something false for true, we are engaging what is, at least from one angle, our most astonishing human capacity: the ability to access ways the world is not but might have been. It's only because we can understand what it would be for the world to be different from the way it is—only because we have epistemic access to possible worlds, if you like—that we can build idealizations. And in building idealizations, truth matters in at least three ways.

First, it matters because, in pursuing Vaihinger's "as if," we need to be able to grasp what it would be for something that isn't so to be true. Second, it matters because the defense of idealization depends on its being true that the models we build are useful for some purpose. And third, it matters because, in identifying the purpose in question, we need to grasp what it would be for the purpose to be achieved: to know, once more, what a world would be like in which something that is not, in fact, true were true. So the kind of truth that matters most for agents whose psychological lives are stocked with the sorts of idealizing models I have been discussing is not just truth in the actual world, as it is, but truth in possible worlds, ways the universe might have been; or if you are a skeptic about those, then let us just say that what matters is the truth about what is possible. Which is why I think it is a good thing, as I said at the start, that we philosophers have a soft spot for truths, even if we have discovered that many of the most exciting and important things we think and say are not, strictly speaking, true at all.

Notes

Acknowledgments

Index of Names

Notes

Preface

1. Sarah-Jane Leslie, "Generics Articulate Default Generalizations," in *Recherches Linguistiques de Vincennes: New Perspectives of Genericity at the Interfaces*, ed. A. Mari (Paris: Presses Universitaire de Vincennes, 2012), 25–45.

2. I am very grateful for the detailed responses to an earlier manuscript from both readers for Harvard University Press. One reader was anonymous. The other was Jason Stanley, who kindly revealed himself to me. It was he who prodded me to acknowledge this presupposition of mine. I will try to acknowledge as his, by name, some of the many points where he assisted me. When I need to refer to the anonymous reader I shall call him or her just that.

3. David Hume, *A Treatise of Human Nature*, ed. L. A. Selby-Bigge (Oxford: Clarendon Press, 1888), 469.

4. "'Hier muss jedenfalls Etwas wahr sein! Der consensus sapientium beweist die Wahrheit.'— Werden wir heute noch so reden? Dürfen wir das?" Friedrich Nietzsche, *Götzen-Dämmerung* (Seattle: CreateSpace Independent Publishing Platform, 2015), 11.

5. Here I am repeating clarifications elicited from me at the Centre for Research in the Arts, Social Sciences and Humanities (CRASSH) seminars at the University of Cambridge in response to a question from Huw Price. The view that all truth is a kind of fiction I take to be the thesis of his *Naturalism without Mirrors* (Oxford: Oxford University Press, 2011). The view about morality I have in mind is some version of the one endorsed by Simon Blackburn in *Essays in Quasi-Realism* (Oxford: Oxford University Press, 1993).

1. Useful Untruths

1. Hans Vaihinger, *The Philosophy of "As If": A System of the Theoretical, Practical and Religious Fictions of Mankind*, trans. C. K. Ogden (New York: Harcourt, Brace, and Co., 1924), xxxiii–xxxiv.

2. Arthur Fine, "Fictionalism," *Midwest Studies in Philosophy* 18 (1993): 1–18.

3. As Paul Guyer pointed out to me in Baltimore, most contemporary Kant scholars would say that Vaihinger exaggerates the similarities of his view to Kant's.

4. William James, *Pragmatism: A New Name for Some Old Ways of Thinking* (New York: Longmans, Green, and Co., 1907), 45–46.

5. Charles S. Peirce, "How to Make Our Ideas Clear," *Popular Science Monthly* 12 (January 1878): 286–302. Beatrice Kobow, who taught me a great deal about Vaihinger during conversations in and around the CRASSH seminars, pointed out that there's no evidence that Vaihinger was directly aware of the work of the American pragmatists (or vice versa). And because his original ideas were sketched in his dissertation in 1877, they were essentially already in place when Peirce published "The Fixation of Belief" (*Popular Science Monthly* 12 [November 1877]: 1–15), which William James regarded as the first public formulation of his pragmatism (James, *Pragmatism*, 46).

6. Vaihinger, *Philosophy of "As If,"* 15. (In all quotes from Vaihinger, any italics are his.)

7. Ibid., 218–219.

8. Ibid., 72.

9. Ibid., 16.

10. Ibid., 17.

11. Ibid., 20.

12. Ibid., 20. Notice that Vaihinger here insists on exactly the point I made earlier: he is interested in the *knowing* use of untruth, not in deception or self-deception.

13. Ibid., xii, xiii, 42.

14. See, for example, Ernan McMullin, "Galilean Idealization," *Studies in History and Philosophy of Science*, Part A, 16, no. 3 (1985): 247–273; and Michael Weisberg, *Simulation and Similarity* (New York: Oxford University Press, 2013), 99–103.

15. Vaihinger, *Philosophy of "As If,"* 24.

16. Jason Stanley pointed me to a very interesting recent discussion in an unpublished paper by Adam Elga and Agustín Rayo titled "Fragmentation and Information Access," March 2015, which I read on Elga's website in September 2016 (https://www.princeton.edu/~adame/papers/fragment/fragmentation-and-information-access-2015-04-08.pdf). This paper offers a detailed defense of one way of handling the fact that we access different pictures of the world in different contexts. I accept the strategy here in Chapter 2 but don't explore the details of its implementation as they do.

17. David Lewis, "Logic for Equivocators," *Noûs* 16, no. 3 (1982): 431–441.

18. "The multiplicity of models is imposed by the contradictory demands of a complex, heterogeneous nature and a mind that can only cope with few variables at a time; by the contradictory desiderata of generality, realism, and precision; by the need to understand and also to control; even by the opposing esthetic standards which emphasize the stark simplicity and power of a general theorem as against the richness and diversity of living nature." Richard Levins, "The Strategy of Model Building in Population Biology," in *Conceptual Issues in Evolutionary Biology*, ed. Elliott Sober (Cambridge, MA: MIT Press, 1984), 41 [originally published in *American Scientist* 54, no. 4 (1966)]; and see Weisberg's discussion in *Simulation and Similarity*, 156–158.

19. Nancy Cartwright, *The Dappled World* (Cambridge: Cambridge University Press, 1999), 184.

20. Ibid., 50.

21. To avoid a possible misunderstanding, I should say that I am not relying here on a distinction between knowing that and knowing how (to use the theory). The knowledge that one can apply a certain formalism in a certain way to predicting the behavior of lasers, say, is not know-how: it's propositional knowledge. Earlier, I mentioned David Lewis's partitioned beliefs about how streets were laid out—his two maps of Princeton.

Elga and Rayo suggest, plausibly, that something like this fragmentation obtains when we distinguish between propositional knowledge, which may repose in abstract principles, and the practical knowledge involved in the application of such principles. They write, "in general, the difference between having knowledge-that and knowledge-how amounts to the difference between having information available for one sort of action, and having it available for another." Elga and Rayo, "Fragmentation and Information Access," 15–16.

22. Mathias Frisch, *Inconsistency, Asymmetry, and Non-Locality: A Philosophical Investigation of Classical Electrodynamics* (New York: Oxford University Press, 2005), 14. For the variety of considerations that are relevant to theory evaluation according to Kuhn, see Margaret Masterman, "The Nature of a Paradigm," in *Criticism and the Growth of Knowledge*, ed. I. Lakatos and A. Musgrave (Cambridge: Cambridge University Press, 1970), 59–90.

23. The anonymous reader argued that I was wrong here, because I presupposed that "treating something as true" involves believing it. As I will argue in more detail later, when discussing make-believe at the end of Chapter 2, I do not think this is so. Still, there is indeed no strict

contradiction between thinking it appropriate to act as one would act if one believed that not-*p*, in a certain specific context, while in fact believing that *p*. (To take the simplest case, I can tell you that not-*p*, which is what I would do if I believed that not-*p*, while believing *p*. That is what we do in the case of the murderer at the door, which Kant made famous. Even if, like Kant, and unlike me, you think it wrong to lie in these circumstances, you must grant it is certainly possible to do so.)

24. In standard semantics for possible worlds, there is only one impossible and one necessary world. For a recent discussion of the issues here, see Daniel P. Nolan, "Impossible Worlds," *Philosophy Compass* 8, no. 4 (2013): 360–372. (Thanks to Jason Stanley for this reference.)

25. It is a familiar point about "accepting" a theory, that this means being willing to use it for certain purposes. It is consistent, therefore, with thinking that it is false—that is, with not believing it.

26. Michael Weisberg, elaborating on what he terms "multiple-models idealization," offers the striking example of how the U.S. National Weather Service uses three different models, with different sets of idealizing assumptions, in order to come up with the most reliable forecasts it can. Weisberg, *Simulation and Similarity*, 103.

27. Vaihinger, *Philosophy of "As If,"* 5.

28. Bas van Fraassen, *The Scientific Image* (Oxford: Oxford University Press, 1980), 12. Van Fraassen doesn't deny that scientific models make claims about the underlying reality; he claims only that it is the empirical adequacy—not the truth—of those claims that matters.

29. Rae Langton, in the CRASSH seminars, raised the objection that this account might justify sexist or racist beliefs, given that such beliefs help men control women, or one race control another. Note, first, that the system of beliefs that underlies sexism or racism includes many elements that are *not* helpful in controlling the world. Racism and sexism both involve beliefs about human biology that are false in ways that make them unhelpful in medicine. And, as Vaihinger wrote (*Philosophy of "As If,"* 45), "We shall indeed have at every step to oppose bad fictions, just as formerly bad hypotheses were opposed." In writing about the role of fictions in upholding an ethical life, he had a clear way of opposing such harmful fictions. Finally, the role of these noxious beliefs in sustaining oppression is not that a person who has them is thereby able to control the oppressed. It is, rather, that the widespread *acceptance* of these beliefs, by men and women, blacks and whites, helps sustain

oppression, allowing members of the dominant class to control those of the subaltern group hegemonically, with the collaboration or consent of the oppressed. For Vaihinger, the mechanism by which having the as-if belief helps a person control the world is by way of her having it, not by way of her getting it widely accepted by others. This distinction will come up again in Chapter 3.

30. This point was borne in on me by Hugh Mellor at the CRASSH seminars.

31. Henry Thomas Buckle, *Introduction to the History of Civilization in England* (London: George Routledge and Sons, 1904), 867; see also the earlier discussion at 806.

32. Later in this chapter, at the end of the section "Sweet Mystery of Life," I will consider how we might know that this was the right explanation. Let me add that Vaihinger doesn't seem to be clear that complexity is relative to our cognitive capacities in this way.

33. Ronald Laymon ventures that "we have what is essentially an optimization problem: the balancing of descriptive accuracy against mathematical tractability." Laymon, "Experimentation and the Legitimacy of Idealization," *Philosophical Studies: An International Journal for Philosophy in the Analytic Tradition* 77, nos. 2/3 (1995): 353–375.

34. Friedrich Albert Lange, *Die Geschichte des Materialismus und Kritik seiner Bedeutung in der Gegenwart*, 2nd ed. (Iserlohn: Verlag Von K. Baedeker, 1873–1875).

35. Vaihinger, *Philosophy of "As If*," 84.

36. Richard Braithwaite, "An Empiricist's View of the Nature of Religious Belief," in *The Philosophy of Religion*, ed. Basil Mitchell (Oxford: Oxford University Press, 1970), 72–91. (This is not such a new idea in the Christian tradition. Saint Paul, after all, says that we "see through a glass, darkly" [1 Cor 13:12].)

37. Vaihinger, *Philosophy of "As If*," 109.

38. Shimon Edelman, *Computing the Mind* (New York: Oxford University Press, 2008), 65.

39. See Gualtiero Piccinini, "The First Computational Theory of Mind and Brain: A Close Look at McCulloch and Pitts's 'Logical Calculus of Ideas Immanent in Nervous Activity,'" *Synthese* 141, no. 2 (2004): 175–215. "Before McCulloch and Pitts, neither Turing nor anyone else had used the mathematical notion of computation as an ingredient in a theory of mind and brain," he notes. But their approach was, he says, presaged in the work by Nicolas Rashevsky, who led the University of Illinois at Chicago's Committee on Mathematical Biology, which McCulloch became acquainted with when he moved to the

university. Rashevsky was an enthusiast for simplified idealized models in biology, defending them on analogy with idealization-rife theoretical physics. Biology, too, could have its billiard balls; he called for "systematic mathematical biology, similar in aim and structure to mathematical physics" (Piccinini, "First Computational Theory," 182–183). And compare Michael Marsalli's fine "McCulloch-Pitts Neurons" module at the Mind Project Curriculum: http://www.mind.ilstu.edu/curriculum /modOverview.php?modGUI=212.

40. Warren H. McCulloch and Walter S. Pitts, "A Logical Calculus of the Ideas Immanent in Nervous Activity," *Bulletin of Mathematical Biophysics* 5 (1943): 115–133, quotation on 118.

41. Ibid., 132.

42. James A. Anderson notes, "Given the state of neurophysiology in 1943, when the ionic and electrical basis of neural activity was unclear, the approximations were much more supportable than they are now." Still, he observes that "two-valued neurons are still used in the current neural network literature because of their convenience for many applications and their nice interface with digital electronics and formal logic." Anderson, *An Introduction to Neural Networks* (Cambridge, MA: MIT Press, 1995), 51, 60.

43. "When an axon of cell A is near enough to excite a cell B and repeatedly or persistently takes part in firing it, some growth process or metabolic change takes place in one or both cells such that A's efficiency, as one of the cells firing B, is increased." Donald Hebb, *The Organization of Behavior* (New York: Wiley and Sons, 1949), 62.

44. Intentions, too, being *about* things, are intentional, as a result: but intentionality isn't just a matter of having intentions!

45. Of course with people we're at least as interested in understanding what they have already done as we are in predicting what they'll do in the future. But in this context, I think all Dennett needs to say is that making an act intelligible is a matter of seeing that it would have been predictable.

46. Daniel Dennett, *Intuition Pumps and Other Tools for Thinking* (New York: W. W. Norton, 2013), 79.

47. This allows him to respond to those Creationists who think that nature shows evidence of design: "It does. But not by a Creator." It also irritates a good number of those who think the right response to the Creationist is to say Darwin showed how you could have adaptation without design.

48. "In crossing a heath, suppose I pitched my foot against a stone, and were asked how the stone came to be there, I might possibly answer, that, for any thing I knew to the contrary, it had lain there for ever; nor would it, perhaps, be very easy to show the absurdity of this answer. But suppose I had found a watch upon the ground, and it should be inquired how the watch happened to be in that place, I should hardly think of the answer which I had before given, that, for any thing I knew, the watch might have always been there. . . . This mechanism being observed, (it requires indeed an examination of the instrument, and perhaps some previous knowledge of the subject, to perceive and understand it; but, being once, as we have said, observed and understood,) the inference, we think, is inevitable, that the watch must have had a maker." William Paley, *Natural Theology* (1802; reprint, New York: Oxford University Press, 2008), 7–8.

49. Dennett, *Intuition Pumps*, 96.

50. Ibid., 97.

51. Ibid., 234.

52. Ian Hacking, *Representing and Intervening* (New York: Cambridge University Press, 1983), 23 (italics in original).

53. And, yes, I have noticed that doubting that we have beliefs looks like something we couldn't

really do if we had no beliefs, because doubting that p would ordinarily involve disbelieving it.

54. G. W. F. Hegel, *Elements of the Philosophy of Right*, ed. Allen Wood, trans. H. B. Nisbet (Cambridge: Cambridge University Press, 1992), 23.

55. S. Baron-Cohen, A. M. Leslie, and U. Frith, "Does the Autistic Child Have a 'Theory of Mind'?," *Cognition* 21, no. 1 (1985): 37–46, doi:10.1016/0010-0277(85)90022-8.PMID 2934210.

56. Paul Churchland, *Scientific Realism and the Plasticity of Mind* (Cambridge: Cambridge University Press, 1979).

57. "Par ma foi! il y a plus de quarante ans que je dis de la prose sans que j'en susse rien, et je vous suis le plus obligé du monde de m'avoir appris cela." (By my faith, for more than forty years I have been speaking prose without knowing anything about it and I am more obliged than anyone in the world to you for having taught me that.) Molière, *Le Bourgeois Gentilhomme*, act 2, scene 4.

58. In *Simulation and Similarity*, Michael Weisberg elaborates just such a taxonomy of what he calls "representational ideals" (105–109). They include completeness, simplicity, and generality (in various senses). In his view, while Galilean idealization aspires to completeness, "minimalist idealizers" are concerned not with truth or accuracy but with identifying "minimal models, discovering

the core factors responsible for the target phenomenon" (111). Those models have explanatory power missing from, for example, black-box models that may have great predictive value. In short, Galilean idealizations, which aim at completeness, will "abate with the progress of science" (103), but when an idealization aims to capture "core features of their targets, to enhance generality or simplicity at all costs, or to maximize predictive accuracy, idealization may be permanent" (113).

59. See Catherine Elgin, "Understanding and the Facts," *Philosophical Studies* 132, no. 1 (2007): 33–42. For her understanding is not "factive," and idealizations may "exemplify features they share with the facts" (33). Robert W. Batterman, exploring case studies in molecular and fluid dynamics, argues that "continuum idealizations are explanatorily ineliminable." Batterman, "Idealization and Modeling," *Synthese* 169, no. 3 (2009): 427. De-idealizing may actually detract from the understanding we get from "a minimal model," which most economically captures the essential physics. Michael Strevens argues, "In certain kinds of deterministic systems, some phenomena are better explained probabilistically than deterministically—in which case you will have a deterministic and a probabilistic model

for the same phenomena, the first of which is predictively better, the second explanatorily better." Strevens, "Depth: Three Interesting Theses," http://www.strevens.org/depth/three theses. For kindred reasons, Paul Teller speaks of the "twilight of the perfect model model." Teller, "Twilight of the Perfect Model Model," *Erkenntnis* 55, no. 3 (2001): 393–415.

60. Michael Strevens, *Depth: An Account of Scientific Explanation* (Cambridge, MA: Harvard University Press, 2008), 311–320.

2. A Measure of Belief

1. D. H. Mellor, *The Matter of Chance* (Cambridge: Cambridge University Press, 1971).

2. Michael Strevens, "A Closer Look at the 'New' Principle," *British Journal for the Philosophy of Science* 46 (1995): 545–561.

3. Fortunately, Ramsey has many fans, some of whom, like Hugh Mellor, showed up for the CRASSH seminars. For them a word of warning here. I am going to use some of Ramsey's ideas in ways he didn't and wouldn't have. So the two main ideas I'm drawing from him are inspiration for what follows, not the implementation of a Ramsey-like program.

4. See Frank P. Ramsey, "Theories," in *Frank Plumpton Ramsey: Philosophical Papers*, ed. D. H. Mellor (Cambridge: Cambridge University Press, 1990), 112–136. The approach was independently discovered by Rudolf Carnap. It seems to have been Carl Hempel who first referred to the approach as involving "Ramsey sentences." See Stathis Psillos, *Scientific Realism: How Science Tracks Truth* (Abingdon, U.K.: Routledge, 1999), 48 and following pages. The great anthropologist was Evans-Pritchard, who spoke of the web of belief in his ethnography of the Azande: "In this web of belief every strand depends upon every other strand, and a Zande cannot get out of its meshes." E. E. Evans-Pritchard, *Witchcraft, Oracles and Magic among the Azande* (Oxford: Clarendon Press, 1937), 194.

5. If our folk psychology is inconsistent, we'll need to tidy it up before we can do this, otherwise we'll know in advance that there are no occult mental states, since no ordered n-tuple will satisfy the open sentence open-M.

6. You might need to add "causes" as one of your "logical" terms.

7. See the papers on probability in Ramsey, *Philosophical Papers*, 52–109.

8. The classical representation theorems don't pick out a single probability function (and they don't

define a unique assignment of utilities either). So there is much of great interest to be said about how we should interpret the mathematical facts here, and what sensible ways, if any, are available to get us where we would presumably like to be, which is to a unique degree for every belief. The problem I want to discuss, though, doesn't depend on any of these details. So, in what follows, I will just assume that we have found a way to assign unique values to subjective probabilities. As so often, then, I too am idealizing.

9. Elizabeth Anscombe, *Intention* (1957; reprint, Cambridge, MA: Harvard University Press, 2000), 68.

10. See Anthony Appiah, *For Truth in Semantics* (Oxford: Blackwell, 1986), chap. 4. It is a hard question, which I will sidestep, exactly what counts as a suitably "disciplined" connection. This was where the conversations in Vienna led some people to verificationism, which most of us now think was a mistake.

11. This paragraph picks up points made by Jane Heal, Henrietta Moore, and Tim Button at CRASSH.

12. Amos Tversky, "Intransitivity of Preferences," *Psychological Review* 76 (1969): 37–40.

13. Michael J. Wood, Karen M. Douglas, and Robbie M. Sutton, "Dead and Alive: Beliefs in

Contradictory Conspiracy Theories," *Social Psychological and Personality Science* 3 (2012): 767–773. (And yes, I know this is not how superposition really works.)

14. R. C. Jeffrey, *The Logic of Decision* (New York: McGraw-Hill, 1965).

15. See Christopher Cherniak, *Minimal Rationality* (Cambridge, MA: Bradford Books, 1986); and my brief review of it: Anthony Appiah, *Philosophical Review* 99 (January 1990): 121–123.

16. For more on computational structure and processes, see chapter 4 of Anthony Appiah, *Assertion and Conditionals* (Cambridge: Cambridge University Press, 1985).

17. Nancy Cartwright, *How the Laws of Physics Lie* (Oxford: Oxford University Press, 1983), 111.

18. It is important, on this view of what "normal" means here, that there should not be a causal law that entails that there will always be some process interfering: otherwise there would be no true counterfactual to the effect that the agent would perform as the functionalist theory requires if a certain factor were absent. And it is because of this that the fact that a system never behaves as the functionalist theory requires is evidence that it is not an agent: for that is evidence that there are no such true counterfactuals.

19. For example, among my set of feasible computations is one that takes me from the belief that John is coming to the belief that it is not the case that he is not coming. And I am capable of applying this computation to any belief, providing it is not too structurally complex. This fact is reflected in the decision theory by the theorem: $p(S) = p(\sim(\sim S))$. It is the fact that I apply computations of the form of double-negation elimination—even if neurophysiological malfunctions or mere structural complexity will sometimes produce the wrong answer—that makes this theory a proper reflection of what I would do if computationally perfect.

20. I think Colin McGinn made this suggestion to me many years ago. There is going to be a technical problem here that has to do with beliefs (and desires) whose contents are about times. The problem arises most clearly when the belief about times is an indexical belief. (Because all action must be connected to representations by way of the "essential indexicals"—I, now, here—there will always be some such beliefs to deal with.) We cannot allow indefinitely greater amounts of time to the agent to calculate the significance of her belief that it will be eight o'clock: give her enough time and she will believe it is past eight o'clock before she

has made up her mind what to do. Many beliefs and desires are aimed at particular times—I want to be outside the cinema at eight tonight, because I believe my friend will be there at that time—so allowing indefinitely long to calculate will not lead to a greater degree of conformity to the requirements of the Economists' Model; in this sort of case, what is required is to speed computation up. There might seem to be a problem here: for though allowing more time is likely to lead toward the right result (so that it is true that the right result is more likely, *ceteris paribus*, if the computations are carried out faster), the increase in the *number* of computations is likely, as a matter of fact, to increase, rather than decrease the likelihood of computational error. What we want to do, then, is to increase the speed of computation in our counterfactual circumstances while holding error down. But this isn't the same sort of theoretical difficulty. For although it is *a priori* true that computations take time, there seems no reason to suppose that it is *a priori* true that any particular set of computations should produce error. The counterfactual hypothesis that there are no errors is thus not one to which we need assign probability 0. Indeed, it is plausible that agents only have finite numbers of actual beliefs and desires, provided we are not dealing with those mathematical beliefs that they are able to generate out of the finite stock of beliefs that defines their mathematical competence, and therefore we may, in general, suppose that there is a finite set of computations that would, if carried out, have led to the right propositions being determined as most-preferred. And then the hypothesis that that set of computations could have been carried out very fast indeed, though counterfactual (and perhaps even physically impossible), is at least only *a posteriori* false.

21. Timothy Williamson, *Knowledge and Its Limits* (Oxford: Oxford University Press, 2000), 209–212; R. K. Shope, "The Conditional Fallacy in Modern Philosophy," *Journal of Philosophy* 75 (1978): 397–413. I'm grateful to Jason Stanley for insisting that I needed to say something about this issue.

22. Normally we give *a priori* truths probability 1 and *a priori* falsehoods 0 when we're constructing subjective probability functions. That means we don't really have a way of representing someone who believes one of those falsehoods or disbelieves one of those truths.

23. I am conscious that this will seem to many too cursory a treatment of these Shope problems, on

which there is now a considerable literature. My object here isn't to solve all the problems of the form of idealization I've proposed. I identify what I think is a related difficulty in note 27 below.

24. Christopher Peacocke, *Thoughts: An Essay on Content* (Oxford: Basil Blackwell, 1986), 3.

25. Ibid., 6–7.

26. There is an oft-told story, alas apocryphal, about an expert in decision theory who was considering an offer to move from one university to another. A colleague suggested that he should simply use the theory. "Don't be silly," the Great Man replied. "This is serious."

27. Jason Stanley made me see that this feature of my proposal—that it was more Fregean than possible-worlds-based—needed to be clarified. Not that my view is one that Frege would have endorsed, because he would have denied that mathematical truth was essentially "about" formal properties of representations. For a recent discussion of the pros and cons of the various options here, see the debate between Stanley and David Chalmers: Jason Stanley, "Constructing Meanings," *Analysis* 74, no. 4 (2014): 662–676; David Chalmers, "Frontloading and Fregean Sense: Reply to Neta, Schroeter and Stanley," *Analysis* 74, no. 4 (2014): 676–697. The proposals they are discussing are in David

Chalmers, *Constructing the World* (New York: Oxford University Press, 2014).

28. From Jorge Luis Borges, "Everything and Nothing," in *Labyrinths: Selected Stories and Other Writings*, ed. Donald A. Yates and James E. Irby (New York: New Directions, 1962), 248, as cited in Kendall Walton, "Fearing Fictions," *Journal of Philosophy* 75, no. 1 (1978), 12.

29. Talk of "props" in this context is one of Kendall Walton's many good ideas; see Walton, *Mimesis as Make-Believe: On the Foundations of the Representational Arts* (Cambridge, MA: Harvard University Press, 1993), 51 and following pages.

30. John Maynard Keynes, *A Tract on Monetary Reform* (London: Macmillan, 1932), 80 (italics in original).

3. Political Ideals

1. John Rawls, *A Theory of Justice* (Cambridge, MA: Harvard University Press, 1971), 8.

2. Ibid., 9.

3. Ibid., 8.

4. Ibid., 4–5.

5. Laura Valentini, "Ideal vs. Non-ideal Theory: A Conceptual Map," *Philosophy Compass* 7/9 (2012): 654–664, doi: 10.1111/j.1747-9991.2012.00500.x.

6. As John Simmons pointed out in "Ideal and Non-ideal Theory," *Philosophy and Public Affairs* 38, no. 1 (2010): 5–36, there are two rather different kinds of noncompliance that Rawls considers. One is the result of deliberate refusal to apply the principles of justice (this he calls "deliberate non-compliance"), and one is the result of unfortunate circumstances, as when a society is too poor to guarantee basic liberty rights (this he calls "unfortunate non-compliance"). Valentini is considering a kind of deliberate noncompliance on the part of individuals.

7. Elizabeth Anderson, *The Imperative of Integration* (Princeton, NJ: Princeton University Press, 2013), 5; Charles W. Mills, "'Ideal Theory' as Ideology," *Hypatia* 20, no. 3 (2005): 165–184. I'm grateful to Jason Stanley for urging me to consider the relevance of this literature. See also his own work on ideology in Jason Stanley, *How Propaganda Works* (Princeton, NJ: Princeton University Press, 2016). For a defense of Rawls's applicability to the project of racial justice, see Tommie Shelby, "Race and Ethnicity, Race and Social Justice: Rawlsian Considerations," *Fordham Law Review* 72, no. 5 (2004): 1697–1714; cf. Mills, "Retrieving Rawls for Racial Justice? A Critique of Tommie Shelby," *Critical Philosophy*

of Race 1, no. 1 (2013): 1–27; and Shelby, "Racial Realities and Corrective Justice: A Reply to Charles Mills," *Critical Philosophy of Race* 1, no. 2 (2013): 145–162.

8. Robert Nozick, *Anarchy, State, and Utopia* (New York: Basic Books, 1974), 151.

9. Ibid., 152.

10. It is probably worth stressing that my commitment to the view that we can separate the epistemic from the ethical in the last analysis does not entail that one cannot inquire about the politics of idealization. It is always possible to ask about what interests are advanced by the way a theory excludes things that are true and includes things that are false. Hence the charge that could be made about the scanting treatment, in *Anarchy, State and Utopia*, of the reality that so many transfers of property historically have violated the norms Nozick defends. On his own account, all the work of thinking about distribution must be done by the very principles of rectification he does not develop. (As his friend, I can affirm that Nozick himself cared a great deal about undoing historical injustice.) Charles Mills remarks that Nozick's principle of rectificatory justice was in principle "very radical, indeed revolutionary," in that there "could hardly be a greater and more

clear-cut violation of property rights in U.S. history than Native American expropriation and African Slavery." He therefore wonders why this implication has been ignored in the secondary literature: "Whence this silence, considering that not even the mental effort of doing a Rawlsian race-behind-the-veil job is required?" See Mills, "'Ideal Theory' as Ideology," 180.

Note that Mills follows Onora O'Neill in preferring abstraction—in which particulars are merely "bracketed"—to idealization. See Onora O'Neill, "Abstraction, Idealization, and Ideology in Ethics," in *Moral Philosophy and Contemporary Problems*, ed. J. D. G. Evans (Cambridge: Cambridge University Press, 1987), 55–69. It is a distinction that readers of Vaihinger will find difficult to sustain. Critics of ideal theory, on closer inspection, often aren't eschewing idealization *tout court*, by whatever name. Once again, which idealizations are to be made depends on what we're interested in, on what our purposes are. Theorists focused on class-based injustices may be quite content with the idealizations of *Das Kapital* (in which the economy could be divided into two parts, production and consumption, and society into capitalists and workers, etc.); a usable conception of patriarchy or white supremacy may itself entrain idealizations. I will say more about the idealizations of non-ideal theory later. There is always, inevitably, the question of whose ox is being gored, or, rather, idealized away.

11. See my summary of Dworkin's proposal in Kwame Anthony Appiah, "Equality of What?" (review of Ronald Dworkin, *Sovereign Virtue: The Theory and Practice of Equality* [Cambridge, MA: Harvard University Press, 2000]), *New York Review of Books* 48, no. 7 (April 26, 2001): 63–68. I make various other objections to this idealization there.

12. I am grateful to the anonymous reviewer for noting that Rawls's account requires mere psychological possibility. Regarding the idealized nature of the original contractors, see Rawls, *A Theory of Justice*, 128, 143.

13. *Defending* a practice by noticing the *benefits* of full compliance is very different from *opposing* a practice by noticing the *downside* of full noncompliance. We often argue that someone should not do something by asking, "What if everyone did that?" "Your shoplifting that candy bar is indeed pretty harmless, but what if everyone did that?" But this form of argument is enthymematic. What noticing the results of full noncompliance does is draw attention to the benefits of pretty-full compliance. And the

reason one should comply isn't that the world would be much worse if one didn't, but that compliance is one's fair share of sustaining a practice from which one benefits. I say more about this below.

14. Utopias both real and fictional have proposed worlds in which the care of children is undertaken collectively. But this involves imagining a situation in which people *recognize* no special obligations to their own children—a counterfactual world—not a counter-normative world in which everything else is much as it is but people *have* no such obligations.

15. The discussion here was shaped especially by the contributions of Angela Breitenbach, Tim Button, and Rae Langton at CRASSH.

16. Another option is to agree that it's always wrong to lie, but recognize that this wrong can be trumped by graver wrongs: inflicting needless emotional distress, say, or exposing someone to danger.

17. G. E. M. Anscombe, "Modern Moral Philosophy," *Philosophy* 33, no. 124 (January 1958): 10.

18. Philip Pettit, "The Cunning of Trust," *Philosophy and Public Affairs* 24, no. 3 (1995): 202–225.

19. This is one of the more important things I learned from the discussions at CRASSH, from Tim Buttons *inter alios*.

20. Ian Hacking, "Making Up People," *London Review of Books* 28, no. 16 (August 17, 2006): 23–26, http://www.lrb.co.uk/v28/n16/ian-hacking/making-up-people.

21. I'm going to ignore the further complexities introduced by the fact that there are intersex people, whose morphology is neither typically male nor typically female. Here, of course, I am idealizing.

22. That this sexologist has much on his side is confirmed in Simon Goldhill's *A Very Queer Family Indeed: Sex, Religion, and the Bensons in Victorian Britain* (Chicago: University of Chicago Press, 2016), a collective biography of Edward White Benson, Archbishop of Canterbury from 1883 to 1896, and his family. The basic facts are nicely summarized in a blog by Christina Beardsley: "That Minnie / Mary Sidgwick Benson was a lesbian and lived, after Edward's death, with Lucy Tait, the daughter of her husband's predecessor as Primate, has been known for some time. Likewise the fact that some, if not all, of their brilliant children—sons E. F. Benson, A. C. Benson, R. H. Benson, and daughter, Margaret Benson—were also gay." (Though one might want to reserve the word "gay" for people who had the concept.) Christina Beardsley, "Keeping It All in the Family,"

Changing Attitude (blog), June 15, 2011, http://changingattitude.org.uk/archives/3652.

23. "Or, il n'y a point d'homme dans le monde. J'ai vu, dans ma vie, des Français, des Italiens, des Russes, etc.; je sais même, grâces à Montesquieu, qu'on peut être Persan: mais quant à l'homme je déclare ne avoir rencontré de ma vie; s'il existe, c'est bien à mon insu." Joseph de Maistre, *Considérations sur la France* (Lyon: Pélagaud, 1880), 88.

24. My theorist need not think this is true in every case. He might hold, in contrast, that the category "alcoholic" is useful for helping people who have difficulty with their drinking, even if alcoholism turns out, in the end, not to be a scientifically sustainable diagnostic category. Compare the discussion of factitious intellectual virtues at the end of the section on "Staying in Character."

25. I am not endorsing this thought. Perhaps if you have sexual desires for prepubescent children, it will help to label yourself a pedophile and seek assistance in resisting these temptations, rather than trying to characterize your sexuality in all its richness, in ways that will lead you to avoid that task.

26. Daniel C. Russell, "Introduction: Virtue Ethics in Modern Moral Philosophy," in *The Cambridge*

Companion to Virtue Ethics, ed. Daniel C. Russell (Cambridge: Cambridge University Press, 2013), 2–3.

27. Rosalind Hursthouse, *On Virtue Ethics* (Oxford: Oxford University Press, 1999); précis of "honest" is from Hursthouse, "Virtue Ethics," *The Stanford Encyclopedia of Philosophy* (Fall 2003 edition), ed. Edward N. Zalta, http://plato .stanford.edu/archives/fall2003/entries/ethics -virtue/. Other influential expositions of virtue ethics include Julia Annas, *The Morality of Happiness* (New York: Oxford University Press, 1993); Roger Crisp, "Modern Moral Philosophy and the Virtues," in *How Should One Live? Essays on the Virtues*, ed. Roger Crisp (Oxford: Oxford University Press, 1996), 1–18; Philippa Foot, *Natural Goodness* (Oxford: Clarendon Press, 2001); Peter Geach, *The Virtues* (Cambridge: Cambridge University Press, 1977); John McDowell, "Virtue and Reason," *Monist* 62 (1979): 331–550; Michael Slote, *Morals from Motives* (Oxford: Oxford University Press, 2001); and Jay Wallace, *Virtues and Vices* (Ithaca, NY: Cornell University Press, 1978).

28. See Lee Ross and Richard E. Nisbett, *The Person and the Situation* (Philadelphia: Temple University Press, 1991). And see John M. Doris, *Lack of Character: Personality and Moral*

Behavior (Cambridge: Cambridge University Press, 2002), 61, 62. Situationism of this kind, which holds that, in explaining other people's behavior, we routinely underestimate the role of situation and overestimate the role of dispositions, is not to be confused with the "situation ethics" promulgated by the theologian Joseph Fletcher, according to which "all laws and rules and principles and ideals and norms, are only contingent, only valid if they happen to serve love in any situation." Fletcher, *Situation Ethics: The New Morality* (Philadelphia: Westminster Press, 1966), 30.

29. And the contexts in question, as situationist experiments show, can be very peculiar. My favorite example: people are much more generous outside bakeries, with the smell of fresh baked goods in the air, than they are outside unfragrant dry goods stores. R. A. Baron and J. Thomley, "A Whiff of Reality: Positive Affect as a Potential Mediator of the Effects of Pleasant Fragrances on Task Performance and Helping," *Environment and Behavior* 26 (1994): 766–784. Cited in Doris, *Lack of Character*, 30–31.

30. Dworkin, *Sovereign Virtue*, 251.

31. This discussion extends the treatment of these questions I developed in Kwame Anthony

Appiah, *Experiments in Ethics* (Cambridge, MA: Harvard University Press, 2008), chap. 2.

32. Mark Alfano, *Character as Moral Fiction* (New York: Cambridge University Press, 2013), 160 (italics in original).

33. Richard H. Thaler and Cass R. Sunstein, *Nudge: Improving Decisions about Health, Wealth, and Happiness* (New York: Penguin, 2009).

34. Joseph Carens, "Realistic and Idealistic Approaches to the Ethics of Migration," *International Migration Review* 30, no. 1 (1996): 156–170. (I'm grateful to Valentini's "Ideal vs. Non-ideal Theory" for drawing this paper to my attention.)

35. Carens, "Realistic and Idealistic Approaches," 156.

36. Cited at ibid., 157. I'm not sure that Hoffman was right here. Some very demanding moral ideas that almost no one can conform to are powerfully motivating. Consider many of the more demanding religiously based moral views in the world today.

37. Ibid., 158.

38. Ibid., 159. The standard of accepting many more refugees in relation to most states is not one where the United States in fact does especially well, given its resources. In 2015, about seventy countries seem to have had more refugees per 1,000 inhabitants than the United States. Some

of them are rich (Canada, Denmark, Norway), some of them are very poor (Guinea-Bissau, Papua New Guinea, Uganda). Data on refugees per country for 2015 are in tab 1 of this file from the UN High Commissioner for Refugees: http://www.unhcr.org/statistics/mid2015stats.zip. Year 2015 national population figures are here: http://www.nationmaster.com/country-info/stats/People/Population-in-2015.

39. Carens, "Realistic and Idealistic Approaches," 160.

40. Ibid., 162.

41. This is something like the view developed by Liam Murphy in his *Moral Demands in Nonideal Theory* (New York: Oxford University Press, 2000).

42. I should note that I doubt that Rawls's response to the claims of the worst-off justifies the material inequalities we actually have in the world. And, in fact, he thought this, too. He was making an argument for the view that there could be justified material inequalities, not claiming that the actual inequalities in the world were justified.

43. G. A. Cohen, *Rescuing Justice and Equality* (Cambridge, MA: Harvard University Press, 2008).

44. Amartya Sen, *The Idea of Justice* (Cambridge, MA: Harvard University Press, 2009). Sen makes

a number of important arguments against approaches to justice that aim to characterize a universal ideal. In particular he makes the important point that knowing what's best won't generally tell you what's better. "The fact that a person regards the *Mona Lisa* as the best picture in the world does not reveal how she would rank a Picasso against a Van Gogh" (101).

45. These paragraphs owe a great deal to Duncan Bell's contributions to the final CRASSH seminar.

46. See Orlando Patterson, *Freedom in the Making of Western Culture* (New York: Basic Books, 1992).

Acknowledgments

The main arguments of this book made their first appearance together as the three Carus Lectures on "Idealization and Ideals" I gave at the 2013 annual meeting of the American Philosophical Association in Baltimore, Maryland. I am extremely grateful to the Association's Lectures Committee, whose members did me the great honor of inviting me to follow in the footsteps of so many distinguished predecessors, beginning with John Dewey, who gave the inaugural lectures in 1925. Those first Carus Lectures grew into *Experience and Nature,* an ambitious account of Dewey's philosophical method. My aims are less ambitious: these are philosophical explorations, not attempts to adumbrate a whole philosophy. My claims, where controversial, are mostly local, and where wide-ranging, are mostly uncontroversial. But I do hope to get other people interested in a set of questions that has long interested me—questions that the invitation to give these lectures led me to pursue further.

I had begun thinking about idealization many years ago, when I was trying to make sense of the idea that one could use probability in the construction of accounts of meaning. My first book, *Assertion and Conditionals* (1985), advertised itself as an essay in probabilistic semantics, and the relevant forms of probability were so-called subjective probabilities, numbers supposed to reflect the strength of a person's beliefs. As I noted in Chapter 2, applying this idea to actual people seems to require a substantial degree of idealization. I wondered how this was supposed to work, and I said a little about it there, but the treatment I gave soon did not strike me as quite satisfactory. So in the late 1980s I returned to the topic and gave a number of talks at various universities on idealization and subjective probability. I have intellectual debts, I am sure, to people who commented on those talks, although I'm afraid my memory of those conversations is pretty sketchy. I see that I mentioned idealization in *The Ethics of Identity* (2005), where I discussed briefly a more general version of the role played by the assumption of a certain model of rationality in psychological theorizing; and the topic shows up again in a different context in another book I wrote, *Experiments in Ethics* (2008), where I discussed the way in which virtue ethics involves various idealizations of human psychology. My return to the topic was prompted by the invitation to give the Carus Lectures. As you see, I had found the issue arising at the edges of many aspects of my work from the beginnings of my philosophical career. So I thought I would try to pull some of these many strands together.

At the Baltimore meetings I was asked thoughtful and stimulating questions. I got many proposals as to how to alter or improve the argument, and I heard many objections. Since then I have tried out versions of some of these thoughts at Berkeley (as the 2015 Howison Lecture) and in a series of extraordinarily helpful (and enjoyable) seminars at the Centre for Research in the Arts, Social Sciences and Humanities (CRASSH) at Cambridge University. I have tried to take account of many thoughtful comments I received, and wish that I had been able to incorporate even more of them into this book. I have acknowledged in the Notes some particular debts that I do recall. In a life of so much reading and so many conversations, one is bound to be shaped in too many ways to remember, let alone reconstruct.

If you recognize an idea you think you gave me that is unacknowledged, know that you, too, have my gratitude.

Harvard University Press sent an earlier draft of this book out for comments, and I was lucky to get back detailed discussions from two very helpful readers. One, as I mention in the Notes, remained anonymous. The other, Jason Stanley, allowed himself to be made known to me. I am very grateful indeed to both of them, because it was their thoughts that guided my final revisions. They will certainly think that I could have made more changes in light of their criticisms, and they will probably be right. But at some point you have to stop fiddling with the text and let it go. I hope, though, that they will agree with me that they have helped make the book better. I'd also like to thank my editor, Lindsay Waters, both for finding them and for all his other help.

Finally, and as always, Henry Finder, my husband, has been my first and best reader: and only those lucky men and women he has edited can truly know how much that means.

Index of Names